There Once Was a Prophet from Judah

There Once Was a Prophet from Judah

Biblical Limericks for Fun and Prophet

Jeff Carter

Foreword by Joel Landon Watts

RESOURCE *Publications* · Eugene, Oregon

THERE ONCE WAS A PROPHET FROM JUDAH
Biblical Limericks for Fun and Prophet

Resource Publications
An Imprint of Wipf and Stock Publishers
199 W. 8th Ave., Suite 3
Eugene, OR 97401

www.wipfandstock.com

PAPERBACK ISBN: 978-1-5326-3818-3
HARDCOVER ISBN: 978-1-5326-3819-0
EBOOK ISBN: 978-1-5326-3820-6

FEBRUARY 16, 2018

To my wife and kids who *still* love me more than I deserve and whom I love more than I can say – though I'll keep trying.

"It is the test of a responsible religion or theory whether it can take examples from pots and pans and boots and butter-tubs. It is the test of a good philosophy whether you can defend it grotesquely. It is the test of a good religion whether you can joke about it."

G. K. CHESTERTON *ALL THINGS CONSIDERED*

Contents

CONTENTS

Foreword

CHESTERTON, I BELIEVE, SAID that any religion we cannot laugh at, shouldn't be believed. This may sound counter intuitive, but in today's age, maybe laughing at our beliefs will lead to a wonderful examination and a revival of sorts. Or another way to think about holy humor. . . remember the passion plays of medieval times—I know some of you do, because you were there—they were not completely dire tales. I suspect the original languages include a fair amount of humor, especially the Hebrew. How else would you survive exile after exile except for faith in God and some humor along the way?

Don Marquis famously said, "There are three types of limericks: limericks to be told when ladies are present; limericks to be told when ladies are absent but clergymen are present; and LIMERICKS." I suspect most of these would fall into one of those categories or the other. Just. . . well, knowing Jeff somewhat. . . be ready to laugh inwardly, feel bad about it for a moment, and maybe laugh outwardly. You should be ready to learn a little about your boundaries as well. The limericks below represent years of laborious study, working, and reworking until that moment when all humor has been sucked dry off the page. It is okay, however, as that seems to be the goal—to suck dry at the well of humor found in Scripture, until Scripture no longer sucks.

It is my deep honor to present to you—to commend to you—limericks that should be read and included in most of your daily readings. Just, for your sake, and for Jeff's, do not use them in the liturgy. One final note: This is not a bible translation. There is no message here. Just love God, read these limericks, and for the sake of all that is holy—laugh! Laugh, human, laugh!

—Joel Landon Watts

Genesis

Let There Be Light

You may think it exceedingly odd
that in the very beginning God,
starting out on day one,
made light before the sun.
Something about this story is flawed.

Genesis 1:3–19

The Serpent Was Blessed

Quiet your vexed vocalization.
The serpent was no aberration.
The good Lord called it forth
gave it value and worth,
a subtle part of God's creation.

Genesis 1:24–25

Genesis Dilemma

After procreating with my wife,
there are still some commands for this life:
I have to figure out
what it means to rule trout,
owls, and cows. I can't handle this strife!

Genesis 1:28

He Was Really Lonely in that Garden

Adam had to face reality:
while the animals had parity,
he was left all alone
with no one he could bone
unless he tried bestiality.

Genesis 2:18–20

Ohhhh get over it. Limericks are *supposed* to be rude.

Besides, that's nothing compared to what Rabbi Eleazar said about Adam alone in the garden before the creation of Eve. Rabbi Eleazar, a Talmudic sage, interpreted the Genesis story this way: "This teaches us that Adam had intercourse with all the animals and all the beasts, but he was satisfied only when he had intercourse with Eve."[1]

Flesh for My Bone

The first man, Adam, lived all alone
with no one he could count as his own.
The animals could mate
in their natural state,
but for the first man there was none.

So Yahweh became the first surgeon
to make for the man one of his own.
With a wound in his side
Adam said with great pride,
"This one at last is flesh for my bone."

Genesis 2:18–23

1. Eleazar, *B. Yeabamoth* 63a

Well that's a Different Kind of Boner

Was it a rib from the man's sternum
that God used to make the first woman?
Or could it be that God
used a different rod,
and that's why we have no baculum?

Genesis 2:22

I'll give you a minute. Go ahead and look it up. . .

Eat My Dust!

The literalists insist we must
take the Bible at its word, or bust,
but it makes little sense
to get mad and incensed
asserting snakes actually eat dust.

Genesis 3:14

God Doesn't Like Vegetarians

Cain brought an off'ring agrarian
while Abel came with fresh carrion.
God chose Abe's, of the two,
so I think that it's true:
God's biased 'gainst vegetarians.

Genesis 4:3–4

Keep it in the Family

East of Eden, to the Land of Nod,
went the fugitive, Cain, marked by God;

it was there that he wed
and took his wife to bed,
but if she's his sis, this story's flawed!

Genesis 4:17

The Song of the Sword

Lamech said to his wives something bold,
"I am a killer, my blood is cold,
for I am better than Cain,
and if I am slain
I'll be avenged seventy-seven fold!"

Genesis 4:23–24

The Origins of the Nephilim

Now the Sons of God were observing
Earth girls with figures that were curving;
they decided to mate,
an act that sealed their fate.
God said, "Of wrath they're now deserving."

Genesis 6:1–4

Noah's Wife

It's an old joke and very well known,
I think it's funny, it gets a groan.
Tell me now, without strife
the name of Noah's wife.
Here's the punch line: his wife's name was Joan.

Genesis 6:18

Joan *of ark*. . . get it? Joan of Arc. Groan.

Noah's Ark

I wonder how Noah did build it,
that ark, and how the animals fit,
and who fed them each day
with those great bales of hay,
and who shoveled the elephant shit?

Genesis 7:1–5

Noah Was an Angry Drunk

Now may a curse be upon Canaan
for what his father, my son, has done;
he saw me passed out drunk,
naked and in full funk:
so let him be slave to everyone.

Genesis 9:20–25

A Fable

Don't be offended by the label,
but I think the Tower of Babel,
as Genesis describes,
just can't be made to jibe
with history. It is a fable.

Genesis 11:1–9

Blessing the Sons of Abraham

When consid'ring the Arab and Jew
it is very important that you
recall without distress
that the Lord God did bless

Abram's sons—Isaac and Ishmael too.

Genesis 17:20; 25:11

That's No Excuse, Lot

The people of Sodom were rotters,
committed to rape and to slaughters.
But e'en with their abuse
there is still no excuse
for Lot to offer up his daughters.

Genesis 19:1–8

Lot's Wife

Leaving the town, she came to a halt.
Should we blame her and say it's her fault?
For curiosity
to see atrocity
some of *us* should be turned into salt.

Genesis 19:24–26

Biblical Kink

Lot, after leaving Sodom and Zoar
lived in caves with his daughters, both whores.
The girls plied him with drink
then, with biblical kink,
conceived Israel's enemies' ancestors.

Genesis 19:30–38

Abraham Got Lucky

God said to Abraham, "kill your son,
your beloved, you know the one;
take out your bloody knife
and sacrifice his life."
So Abe obeyed without a question.

But good God, and good grief, and God damn!
What the hell's wrong with you, Abraham?
To follow as if blind
a request so unkind?
You're lucky God provided a ram.

Genesis 22

Testify

It was the custom, in days gone by,
to place your hand here under my thigh
to mark a solemn vow,
but be sure to allow
that it really means cupping the guy.

Genesis 24:9; 47:29

In a related note—the English word "Testify" comes from the same root as "Testicle."

Good for Sermons, Bad for Biology

The Bible's good for homiletics
but it says little of genetics.
Jacob's trick with the rods
is demonstrably flawed
and displays questionable ethics.

Genesis 30:25–43

Who Sold Joseph to Whom?

The elder sons of Father Israel,
in a moment less than filial,
sold their brother Jacob
to the first passing mob,
who were, by chance, the sons of Ishmael.

But wait a minute, that isn't right,
there's a slight contradiction in sight.
In one of these lines I
read he was rescued by
a caravan of Midianites.

Genesis 37:28, 36; 39:1

Seed on the Ground

T'was his duty and Onan was bound:
get Tamar pregnant, her belly round.
But Onan didn't care
to produce any heir
and instead spilt his seed on the ground.
Genesis 38:8–9

Onan's story is the perfect. . . seed for limericks.

Thank you, Onan

Oh, Onan, how you do amuse us.
Because of you we get to discuss
whether or not it is
a great sin to spill jizz;
thanks to your *coitus interruptus*.

Genesis 38:9

That's How Mad Cow Disease Got Started, You Know. . .

Pharaoh once had a dream unbenign,
a dream that sent shivers down his spine.
He saw something vile
come up from the Nile:
those cannibalistic river kine.

Genesis 41:1–4 (KJV)

Kine is the only plural form in the English language that does not
share a single letter with its singular—Cow.

The First Socialist

Evangelical apologists
must be well confirmed capitalists
for there are very few
who will admit to you
that Joseph was the first socialist.

Genesis 41

Carry up My Bones from Here

Prince Joseph from his deathbed intones:
"Make for me in Egypt no headstones.
You should do this instead,
when I am cold and dead,
go to the Promised Land with my bones."

Genesis 50:24–25

Exodus

Hebrew Women Are not Like Egyptian Women

Pharaoh instructed all the midwives:
let no Hebrew boys be born alive,
"But our women are strong,
and it never takes long;
they give birth before we arrive."

Exodus 1:15–19

Seriously Understaffed Midwives

It's no wonder that when the Hebrews
came to the time their babies were due
the midwives weren't around,
there were few to be found;
in all Egypt there were only two.

Exodus 1:15, 19

Strike!

What's the book of Exodus about?
Why, it's a labor story, no doubt:
Pharaoh cruelly abused
and exploited the Jews
so they all went on strike and walked out.

Exodus 2–12

No Excuse for Papyrus

That Jochabed did use papyrus
to make an ark for her son Moses
is not a good excuse
for the continued use
of that foul font by the rest of us.

Exodus 2:3

They'll Take the Credit, but Will they Accept the Blame?

The rulers will take credit, no doubt
for good that happens under their clout:
Pharaoh's daughter sent her
maid into the river
then made the claim, "*I* drew Moses out."

Exodus 2:5, 10

Slow of Speech and Tongue

The flames in the bush were aflutter
when Moses first heard God's voice utter
the command to go speak,
but Moses said, "I'm weak
and I st- st- st- st-. . . can't speak well."

Exodus 3:2; 4:10

First! Or Maybe not. . .

In the time of Adam, so they say,
people began to call on Yahweh,
and right up to Moses,

who wrongly supposes,
he was first to use the name that way.

Exodus 6:2–3; Genesis 4:26; 15:7; 27:20

Do Not Have Sexual Relations with your Father's Sister

Hey, hey wait! There's something amiss here:
Amram married his father's sister,
but by *Torah* you can't
copulate with your aunt,
even to conceive Moses, mister!

Exodus 6:20; Leviticus 18:12

Not Helping

Egyptian magicians served their king
by each of the plagues reproducing,
snakes and blood, frogs as well
which caused Pharaoh to yell,
"Dammit, you guys! This isn't helping!"

Exodus 7:11–12, 22; 8:3

Pull My Finger

It is rare that the phrase is invoked,
but when "the finger of God's" provoked
lice is formed up from dust,
the law in stone is thrust,
and demons of Beelzebub get poked.

Exodus 8:19[1]; 31:18; Deuteronomy 9:10; Luke 11:19–20

---

1. Or Exodus 8:15 depending on your translation. The verse numbering for chapters 7 and 8 vary.

Yam Suph

On this point I'd like to intercede,
make the correction the Bible needs;
in Hebrew it's *Yam Suph,*
but a translator's goof
changed the Sea to Red instead of Reeds.

Exodus 10:19

To Roast or To Boil?

The priestly author insists, madam,
that we roast and not boil the lamb,
but Deuteronomy's
author quite disagrees,
'boil it,' he says, 'roasting be damned.'

Exodus 12:9; Deuteronomy 16:7

The verb used in Deuteronomy 16:7 is translated in most every other instance as "boiled" but is deliberately changed by some translations to "cooked" or even "roasted" in this verse to bring it into line with the explicit prohibition on boiling the Passover lamb found in Exodus 12: 9. Meanwhile, 2 Chronicles 35: 13 sees King Josiah roasting *and* boiling the Passover lamb in order to keep both forms of the command, and the Greek Septuagint translation of Deuteronomy 16: 7 has both, "you shall boil *and* roast and eat it."

Flesh Pots

Their flight to the desert was complete
but the Hebrews had nothing to eat,
so they wept and they cried,
"If only we had died
in Egypt where we had potted meat!"

Exodus 16:3

Maybe it's Better not To Know

Manna came at night, but what was it?
No one really knows, we must admit,
but some have suggested
that what was ingested
was the residue of insect spit.

Exodus 16:14–15

That's What You Call an Anachronism

Israel in Sin was hungry, you bet.
So God fed them with manna, no sweat.
This event they did mark,
putting some in the Ark;
only problem: there weren't no Ark yet.

Exodus 16:33–34; Exodus 37

Like a Rolling Stone

Rephidim's rock, so it is written,
followed Israel like a lost kitten;
the rock, as would behove
did pursue out of love
for by Moses it had been smitten.

Exodus 17:1–7

This one is a little complicated to explain but here goes: the Israelites are somewhere near Rephidim which is near Mt. Horeb. They're thirsty, they complain, God tells Moses to strike the rock there with his staff, and they have water. And Moses names the place, "Meribah."

Later, after receiving the *torah*, they leave that place and head to Kadesh (Numbers 20:1–14) where again they are thirsty and complain that they need water. Moses strikes the rock again (a no-no this time) and they have water. And again Moses names the place "Meribah"

This might be an example of one traditional story being told in two different ways, but the Jewish rabbis had a legend that since the rock is named "Meribah" in both places, that it was the same rock and that the rock actually followed the people of Israel from Rephidim to Kadesh.

"And so the well, which was with Israel in the desert, looked like a rock with the size of a sieve, surging and gurgling upward, as from the mouth of this flask, rising with them up on to the mountains and going down with them into the valleys. Wherever the Israelites would encamp, it made camp opposite to them, opposite to the Tent of Meeting."[2]

The Apostle Paul apparently knew of this legendary tradition. He draws from the story of the "rolling stone" in his letter to the church at Corinth: where he mentions the spiritual rock that followed them, and then declares that the rock was Christ. (1 Corinthians 10:4)

The People Quarreled with Moses

Moses, you are such a goddamn putz!
Did you lead us out here to kill us
with hunger and with thirst?
Good grief! You are the worst!
If we grouse it's 'cause we hate your guts.

Exodus 17:2–4

Moses the Dowser

Moses was a bit of a wowzer,
and before you object, note how sir:
he swung his wooden rod,
as instructed by God,
and struck the rock just like a dowser.

Exodus 17:6

2. Tosefta *Sukkah* 3:11

Strike the Rock, Don't Strike the Rock. . .

In Ex'dus seventeen it's okay
for Moses to strike the rock, but hey!
In Numbers twenty when
Moses does it again
he's barred from the Promised Land, *oy vey*!

Exodus 17:6; Numbers 20:8–12

No One Wants to See That

When you construct an altar for prayers
be certain to build it without stairs.
Ascending you'll expose
that what's covered by clothes,
and no one should see your *derrières*.

Or, even worse, it could be your fates
as you worship with all of your mates
to make a great error
as you go up the stairs
and reveal to the crowd your privates.

Exodus 20:25–26

Some Rules for Happy Polygamy

Say your first wife's a bit of a bore,
and now you're looking for something more;
you may take a new wife,
but for all of her life
you must care for the first as before.

Give her the food, and clothing, and rights
just as she had before, with no sleights.
Though you have a new bride,

if the first is denied
she may leave your ass one of these nights.

Exodus 21:10–11

God Loves Artists Best (or at least first. . .)

Of course we know our God will impart
his spirit to fill the human heart,
but the first to be filled
was a man who was skilled
in creating great works of fine art.

Exodus 31:1–6

'Dat Ass

Moses had but one favor to ask,
"Lord, please let your face before me pass."
But Yahweh, he declined;
showed aught but his behind.
"Not my face, but I'll show you my ass."

Exodus 33:18–23

The Veil of Moses

As Moses came down the mountain trail
God's glory on his face did prevail.
The people, filled with fear,
were afraid to draw near
and screamed, "Moses, please put on a veil!"

Exodus 34:29–35

Leviticus

Rabbits Refect

There are some malicious reviewers
who would put the Bible on skewers,
but don't get out of joint
though they may have a point:
rabbits technically aren't cud chewers.

Leviticus 11:3–6

Rabbits do eat their partially digested fecal pellets, a process called refection. This is similar to, but not the same as, rumination or "cud chewing."

Moses Was not an Ornithologist

I know it's silly, that it's absurd
to get hung up on a little word
and there's not much at stake
in this little mistake,
but, dang it all, a bat ain't a bird!

Leviticus 11:13–19

Moses wasn't a chiropterologist, either for that matter.

Four Legged Insects?

Now, let's not set off the powder kegs;
keep the conversation calm, I begs,
but let's question the text
for how many insects
do you know that have only four legs?

Leviticus 11:20

Unclean

A man lies with his woman, and then
he has an emission of semen.
Now they are both unclean,
if you know what I mean,
that's the word. Can I get an amen?

Leviticus 15:18

Yom Kippur

Now don't be so silly or flip or
profane, but today we must skip o'er
food, sex, and leather shoes,
for this is how we Jews
keep and commemorate *Yom Kippur.*

Leviticus 16:29; 23:27

Two Different Materials

I am sorry to say this, my friend,
but our friendship must come to an end;
I must from you withdraw

for you've broken God's law:
your shirt is a poly-cotton blend.

Leviticus 19:19

Does This Apply to Women as Well?

Though it is a book truly revered,
there are parts that are just a bit weird.
Read it; you'll find hidden
among things forbidden
Leviticus bans trimming your beard.

Leviticus 19:27

We Won't Follow this One

Though our Bibles are thumbed and well-worn
we treat this verse with sneers and with scorn.
We may read it, but we
will refuse to agree
to treat foreigners as native born.

Leviticus 19:33–34

No Dwarves!

What in this instruction is unclear?
No one with a defect may come near.
So you should stay at home
if you're a hunch-backed gnome,
God doesn't want you to worship here.

Leviticus 21:18–20

Sorry Lance Armstrong

Though it might make you feel insecure,
if you've had cancer testicular
and your testes were cut
the chapel doors are shut.
On this scripture's quite particular.

Leviticus 21:20; Deuteronomy 23:1

Lex Talionis

The *Lex Talionis* law was good,
for when correctly applied it would
put limits on revenge,
so that no one could binge
on the gouging of eyes, which is rude.

Leviticus 24:20

The Obvious Meaning Can't Be Right

Oh, everyone's a literalist,
that is, at least, until you insist
the Year of Jubilee
is good for you and me,
then that method is quickly dismissed.

Leviticus 25

Private Property

Those who defend private property
as a right giv'n by divinity
truly don't understand

the biblical command
that calls for the Year of Jubilee.

Leviticus 25

It's Okay if They're from Canada

Say I want to buy a slave, okay,
what does scripture on that topic say?
"Your slaves you should accrue
from nations around you."
So I'll get mine from Canada, eh?

Leviticus 25:44

Numbers

Curses!

The Lord said, "If your wife goes astray
bring her to the priest without delay.
He will give her a drink
made of curses in ink
and her sex organs will waste away."

Numbers 5:11–31

Won't That Be Neat!

The Israelites complained, "We want meat."
God was annoyed, so he said, "Fine! Eat!
To your groans I'll submit;
I'll feed you meat till it
leaks out your nostrils. Won't that be neat?!"

Numbers 11:18–20

Don't Ignore This

His story is found in the *Torah*.
It's something you should not ignora:
he rebelled 'gainst Moses,
and that was atrocious,
so the ground devoured old Korah.

Numbers 16:32

Poor Balaam

I should like to point out that Balaam
never, not once, did he regale 'em
except with the true word
that he from Yahweh heard.
Why do we constantly assail 'im?

Numbers 22:2–24:25

Unicorns

So I find myself somewhat forlorn
by Bible translations which are shorn
of that mythical beast
found in the Middle East,
for I believe in the unicorn.

Numbers 23:22; 24:8; Deuteronomy 33:17; Job 39:9–10; Psalm 22:21;
29:6; 92:10; Isaiah 34:7 in the KJV.

That's Certainly Coitus Interrupted

Now Phinehas was zealous of course,
but may have used a bit too much force.
In a moment of zeal
with his spear of firm steel
he skewered the two mid-intercourse.

Numbers 25:6–8

Zelophehad's Daughters

Biblical law was left incomplete
till Zelophehad's daughters could meet
with Moses to request

that their father's bequest
be delivered to them *tout de suite.*

Numbers 27:1–11

Deuteronomy

Give it to a Stranger

If, while you're walking in nature,
you find a carcass, this is danger.
Don't eat what you find dead,
you are pure, so instead
you should give it all to a stranger.

Deuteronomy 14:21

Debt Cancellation

Christians who call for castigation
of those pledging debt cancellation
as part of their campaign
are reminded again
that it's Jubilee realization.

Deuteronomy 15:1

Jubilee

"Let's read the Bible literally,"
they say, "and obey it completely,
except we will leave out
all those verses about
cancelling debts in the Jubilee."

Deuteronomy 15:1–18

Well, that's One Way to Do It

Listen close—here is what we must do,
if to the Bible we would be true,
here's what it has to say
and what we must obey:
There shall be no needy among you.

Though liberals will object and bray,
we should pass a new law straight away
giving cit'zenship to
just the propertied few
and force poor people to go away.

Deuteronomy 15:4

Women Taken in War

You've captured a woman you'd like to wed,
you have clipped her nails, and shaved her head;
give her a new outfit,
let her in mourning sit
then you can finally take her to bed.

Deuteronomy 21:10–13

Another Traditional Biblical Marriage

If you take, from the captives of war,
a wife who is beautiful, she's yours,
and when you've had your way
you may send her away
if you don't want her 'round any more.

Deuteronomy 21:10–14

Ignore that One, Please

If a man has a rebellious son,
here's what the scriptures say must be done:
he should be stoned to death,
till he has no more breath.
I'm glad my father ignored that one.

Deuteronomy 21:18–21

Advice to Young Women

Virgin women, hear and heed me well:
If you are raped, remember to yell.
You must be loud and clear
for if the men don't hear
you'll have to be stoned to death as well.

Deuteronomy 22:23–24

What Does God Have Against Marine Invertebrates?

This is something I can't understand:
why the Ammonites were to be banned.
How could extinct mollusks
be the cause of such fuss,
when they don't even live on the land?

Deuteronomy 23:3–6

The word "Ammonite" can refer to either the people of the ancient Levant descended from Ben-Ammi, the son of Lot, or a type of extinct mollusk. Confusing to be sure. . .

No Spontaneous Orgasms for Soldier Boys

When your soldiers go out on missions
they should be quick with their admissions,
lest a failure result
from that critical fault
of having nocturnal emissions.

Deuteronomy 23:9–11

Step In It

The soldiers should carry in their kit
a tool to turn, and cover their shit;
this they always should do
for Yahweh walks with you
and he doesn't want to step in it.

Deuteronomy 23:12–14

Sounds like Wealth Redistribution to Me

Tell me the truth, and please make it plain;
do not dissemble or confuse my brain.
Do you accept scripture
that would open up your
fields to let someone else eat your grain?

Deuteronomy 23:24–25

Fight Club (no Girls Allowed)

If, two men are engaged in a fight
and the wife of one should, in her spite,
reach out with her hand

to protect her husband,
squeeze his assailant's stones with her might,

you must then, showing her no favor,
cut off her hand, though it should maim her.
For the men must fight fair,
and none should interfere
with this display of manly behavior.

Deuteronomy 25:11–12

Curses!

If you are a recalcitrant git
the Lord will drive thee crazed in thy wit
with scabs and with swelling
too gross to be telling,
and boils on the part where you shit.

Deuteronomy 28:27–28

Be Happy or Else!

Be happy for what Yahweh has done.
Neither grumble nor gripe; do not groan;
for if you should complain,
or speak against his name,
with an iron yoke he'll crush your bones!

Deuteronomy 28:47–48

The Saddest of All Scriptures

How are we to appraise or give worth
to the saddest scriptures on the earth?
It speaks of the mother

who can do naught other
but to hide and eat her afterbirth.

Deuteronomy 28:56–57

Joshua

Quid Pro Quo

Joshua sent spies to Jericho,
gave the mission to them, even though
their plan did constitute
of seeing prostitutes
for a bit of the old *quid pro quo*.

Joshua 2:1–2

What Happened to Jericho?

It's a story I think that you know,
how Joshua fought at Jericho;
the city walls fell flat
and that, they say, was that,
but where did all the evidence go?

Joshua 6

No archeological evidence remains to corroborate the story of Joshua's battle at Jericho. What evidence is available suggests that the destruction at Jericho (one of many successive destructions) happened at an earlier time, well before the time of the story of Joshua's conquest of Canaan.[1]

---

1. Neev and Emery, *Destruction of Sodom, Gomorrah and Jericho*, 103–104.

As Found in the Lost Book of Jasher

As the sun stood still o're Gibeon,
God threw down about a million
hailstones, a right smasher
from the Book of Jashar,
though that work's lost to oblivion.

Joshua 10:12–14

Judges

Thumbs and Big Toes

Adoni-Bezek treated his foes
with viciousness and many cruel blows,
so when the Israelites
captured him in a fight
they dismembered his thumbs and big toes.

Judges 1:4–7

Gullet Is a Funny Word

Fat Eglon, the Moabite king, met
with Ehud, the judge, who was dead set
on murdering the king
but in their brief meeting
Ehud's sword got stuck in the king's gullet.

Judges 3:21–22

Not Bad at All

After Ehud came the man, Shamgar,
a hero of Israel without par;
he used an old ox-goad
to pursue down the road
six hundred Phil'stines—not bad, by gar!

Judges 3:31

Never Let It Be Said

As a king, Abimelech was flawed,
he ran over his subjects roughshod;
at Thebez he was crowned
with a mill-stone thrown down
by a woman whom we should all laud.

Abimelech, he fell down slack-jawed,
asked his page to pierce him with a rod,
"For it cannot be said
when I am good and dead
that I was killed by a lousy broad!"

Judges 9:50–54

Whatever Happened to Tola?

After Abimelech came Tola
to judge Israel and enforce the law;
he judged twenty three years
and the last that we hear
he's in Shamir where worms on him gnaw.

Judges 10:1–2

Most Ghoulish

Jephthah made a vow that was foolish
and kept it because he was mulish;
even though his daughter
was what he would offer,
he made the sacrifice most ghoulish.

Judges 11:29–40

Shibboleth

Jephthah told all the men of his team,
"Here's how we'll find men of Ephraim:
we will give them a test:
say the word *Shibboleth*;
if he can't say it right, you kill 'im."

Judges 12:4–6

Bizarre Behavior for Bees

I don't get it. It's a mystery
that shouldn't be read as history,
for to build a beehive
in what once was alive
would be bizarre behavior for bees.

Judges 14:8

Samson Unhinged

Samson, as a hero, seems unhinged.
On violence and cruelty he binged,
setting foxes on fire
in his rage and his ire;
on the Philistines he'd be revenged!

Judges 15:1–5

The First Suicide Bomber

Would Samson be thought a great leader,
if we saw through his saintly veneer?
We must face the hard fact

that in his final act
he became a suicide bomber.

Judges 16: 23–31

Not Exactly a Love Story

The concubine fled after their fight,
the Levite trailed to prove he was right,
but when threatened by men
who were set upon sin,
he left her to be gang raped all night.

Judges 19

Plunder and Rape Your Way to a Biblical Marriage

The men of Benjamin had no brides
so they armed themselves, set out to ride.
No virgin would escape
as they plundered and raped,
not till enough women were supplied.

Judges 21

Ruth

How Should We Read Ruth's Story?

How then should we interpret Ruth's tale?
Was she a woman by fate assailed,
who then sleeps with her boss
to prevent greater loss?
He promotes her to wife, so all's well. . .

Ruth 1–4

It Wasn't His Feet

The story of Ruth is a real treat,
but don't be fooled, it isn't discreet.
While Boaz was asleep
to his side she did creep,
but she didn't uncover his. . . feet."

Ruth 3:6–8

"Foot" is often used as a euphemism for genitalia in the Bible. "Feet hair" in Isaiah 7:20 is pubic hair, and one pair of the seraph's wings in Isaiah 6 is used to modestly cover their. . . feet. King David encouraged Uriah, home from the front lines of battle to go home and "wash his feet" with his wife Bathsheba (2 Samuel 11: 8).[1]

---

1. Pope. "Euphemism and Dysphemism", 721

First and Second Samuel

Emerods

The Philistines were more than annoyed;
their statue of Dagon was destroyed,
and the folks of Ashdod
were struck with emerods.
That's to say, a case of hemorrhoids.

1 Samuel 5:1–12 (KJV)

Who Killed Goliath?

Goliath of Gath was a tall man
measuring four cubits and a span.
Scripture tries to explain
how he came to be slain
but was it David or Elhanan?

1 Samuel 17; 2 Samuel 21:19

Son-in-Law

Saul didn't want David as his kin
but his daughter was in love with him.
With a plan cold as ice
he settled the bride price
at one-hundred Philistine foreskins.

But David was bold and determined
that the king's approval he would win,
so he went out with his men
to fight once again
and returned with two hundred foreskins.

1 Samuel 18:20–27

Is Saul One of the Prophets, Too?

Overcome by the Spirit of God,
Saul quickly stripped the clothes off his bod,
then went in a frenzy,
like a dervish, till he
came to Ramah. Now isn't that odd?

1 Samuel 19:23–24

Because "Son of a Perverse, Rebellious Woman" Doesn't Have the Same Ring to It

King Saul wanted Jonathan to snitch
on David but there was a slight hitch:
Jonathan was loyal,
so Saul's anger boiled.
"I'll kill him yet, you son of a bitch!"

1 Samuel 20:25–31

Read it in the Living Bible (1972) paraphrase.

Why Bring Him to Me?

David played mad for Abimelech
till the annoyed king said, "what the heck?
He's head-butting the door

and drooling on the floor;
this fool's not dealing from a full deck."

1 Samuel 21:14–16

The Cave of Adullam

David was an outlaw on the lam,
hiding in the Cave of Adullam,
and joining David there,
men with debts and despair;
four hundred men in that cave did cram.

1 Samuel 22:1–2

How to Insult Someone the Biblical Way

You and a friend have started to brawl
and you're strapped for an insult to bawl.
You could always refer
to the biblical slur,
and say he "pisseth against the wall!"

1 Samuel 25:22; 34; 1 Kings 14:10; 16:11; 21:21; 2 Kings 9:8 (KJV)

She Was a Happy Medium

There was a witch who lived in Endor,
who knew the incantations and lore;
in the darkness of nights
she would perform the rites
to bring up the dead spirits once more.

1 Samuel 28

Not Much of a Narrative Arc

Uzza reached out his hand for the ark,
to prevent it from falling, but hark!
For his temerity,
with great celerity,
he died—not much of a narr'tive arc.

2 Samuel 6:6–7

Butt Naked

King David was enraged and aghast;
men he sent to Hanun were harassed.
So that people would scoff,
their beards were shaved half off
and the men were sent back home bare assed.

2 Samuel 10:1–4

Call It What It Is

Some people would the story reshape,
but should we let King David escape?
His sin's not just murder,
but what he did to her.
What he did to Bathsheba's called rape.

2 Samuel 11:1–5

Absalom, oh Absalom!

It reads like a great biblical joke:
Abs'lom got his head stuck in an oak,
entrapped by his long hair

and when Joab got there
with his spear he gave the prince a poke.

2 Samuel 18:9–15

Neither Toenails nor Mustache

Mephibosheth was just a bit rash,
went into hiding fearing backlash;
while he was withdrawn there
forgot personal care
and trimmed neither toenails nor mustache.

2 Samuel 19:24

Who Made Him Do It?

Parts of scripture need to be straightened
because confusion is inflatin'.
David's tale, for instance,
who prompted his census?
Was it God or was it the Satan?

2 Samuel 24:1; 1 Chronicles 21:1

First and Second Kings

Hello Nurse!

When David the king was quite old
he found that he was frequently cold;
though cloaks were piled on
his warmth had all gone,
so his staff made a plan that was bold.

A virgin, a beauty to behold,
into bed with the king would be rolled.
There was nothing debased,
she was perfectly chaste. . .
at least that's how the story was told.

1 Kings 1:1–2

3.14159265358979323...

First Kings measures the value of *pi*
in the temple's "molten sea", but I
am confused; it says three,
and I know this can't be.
I learned the value in junior high.

1 Kings 7:23

What's in the Box?

What was kept in the ark? Just one thing:
Stone tablets of the law and nothing!
Oh, I almost forgot,
manna in a gold pot
and Aaron's staff, but that's everything. . .

1 Kings 8:9; Hebrews 9:4

King Solomon's Navy

The king was rich, but wanted more, see,
so he built himself an argosy,
equipped a fleet of ships
that were launched from their slips
to bring back booty from the high sea.

1 Kings 9:26–28

It Can't Just Be Coincidence!

I've figured it out, just what John meant,
and I have proven my argument.
It is not a blunder;
the Beast's magic number
is the weight of Sol'mon's gold talents!

1 Kings 10:14; Revelation 13:18

700 Wives and 300 Porcupines? That Can't Be Right

Solomon loved the foreign women,
from Moab and Edom to Yemen;
he held fast in his love

despite word from above.
He was warned but he wouldn't listen.

1 Kings 11:1–4

Maybe not the Wisest, After All

Solomon was the wisest of kings
but seven hundred wives wore his rings,
and he had to make time
for all of his concubines.
How did he find time for governing?

1 Kings 11: 3

Maybe that Wasn't the Best Way To Begin

Rehoboam was Solomon's son,
became king when the old man was done;
his first speech was quite rash,
"Dad beat you with a lash,
but I will be using scorpions!"

1 Kings 12: 1–14

Caterwaul

At Carmel the prophets of Ba'al
danced about with a loud caterwaul,
cutting themselves with knives
and screaming for their lives,
"Oh Ba'al, please let the fire fa'all!"

1 Kings 18: 26–29

Punch the Prophet Or Else!

Said the prophet to the man, "Strike me."
Said the man, "I won't, for I like thee."
Said the seer, "A lion
will kill you, no lyin.'"
Do pastors preach from this? Not likely.

1 Kings 20: 35–36

Go Up Baldy!

Elisha was a man to beware,
sensitive about his lack of hair.
When some boys on the way
called out, "go up, Baldy!"
He cursed them to be mauled by she-bears.

2 Kings 2:22–25

Hell's Kitchen

Now Elisha's cook was not so hot,
he cooked with gourds that were filled with rot.
When the men ate his stew
it was chunks that they blew.
Man of God! There is death in the pot!

2 Kings 4: 38–41

Cannibal Mothers Don't Play Fair

She said to me, "Let's eat yours today,
and tomorrow we'll eat mine, okay?"
We boiled my son up,

and on him we did sup,
but now she's hidden her son away.

2 Kings 6: 28–29

He Drives like a Madman

He may have been Israel's king, but you
would be wise the highways to eschew;
for when he took the reins
his chariot caused pain–
there's no one else that drives like Jehu!

2 Kings 9: 20, 30–33

Poultice of Fig

The king was fatally ill, you dig?
So he prayed a prayer, quick as a jig.
Isaiah the prophet,
announced, "He's healed, you bet,
but smear him with a poultice of fig."

2 Kings 20: 1–7

First and Second Chronicles

Ambidextrous

The men that came to join David's band
were the mightiest in all the land;
they were skilled with the sling
and the bow for killing,
shooting from both the left and right hand.

1 Chronicles 12: 1–2

And that's Not Counting the Silver

If a talent's seventy-five pounds
the tale of Solomon's Temple sounds
a little suspicious,
or even fictitious.
Seven plus million pounds of gold? Zounds!

1 Chronicles 22:14

100,000 talents of gold is approximately 3,775 tons or 7,550,000 pounds.[1] Consider also that King David's crown weighed "a talent of gold." 2 Samuel 12: 30 (NIV)

I Believe the Proper Term Is "Prolapsed"

Jehoram was a bad king, no doubt
who led by the apostasy route;

1. Myers, *1 Chronicles*, 152.

he was king for eight years
then he died amid tears
when Yahweh caused his bowels to fall out.

2 Chronicles 21: 4–20

Bloody Smear

Amaziah's army was top tier,
killed 10,000 Edomites at Sier,
but that wasn't enough
so they tossed from a bluff
10,000 more, left a bloody smear.

2 Chronicles 25:12; 2 Kings 14:7

Ezra

Ezra and the Department of Homeland Security

The priests of Israel had heaped up shames,
they'd wedded themselves to foreign dames.
Marrying foreign gals
so offended morals
that Ezra published all of their names.

Ezra 10

Nehemiah

Nehemiah's Agitation

To Nehemiah's agitation
the people of his Jewish nation
were committing a sin
participating in
acts of racial miscegenation.

Nehemiah 13: 23–27

The KKK Opposed Miscegenation Too

Nehemiah was a mean, cruel man,
vexed with the men of Jerusalem;
he yelled and cursed them out,
punched and knocked them about,
just for marrying outside the clan.

Nehemiah 13: 25

Tobit

Almsgiving

Tobit says it with striking starkness:
if you want to preserve your carcass
eliminate all qualms
'bout the giving of alms.
It stops death and trips into darkness.

Tobit 4:10

Apocryphal Fish Stories

Tobias camped along the Tigris;
up from the water leaped a great fish.
An angel said to him,
"Catch that fish; reel it in!
With its offal you can cure illness."

Tobit 6: 2–5

Judith

Blessed Art Thou among Women

I've begun to lament and to wail;
I can't tell which biblical female
is the most highly blessed,
above all of the rest:
Was it Judith, Mary, or Jael?

Judith 13: 23–25, Luke 1: 26–28, Judges 5: 24–27

Esther

I'll Bet They Paid Her in Singles

King Xerxes, drinking wine with his men,
called for the Queen to entertain them.
"Come, Vashti, wear your crown,
but take your fine robes down,
so we can see your beauty again."

Esther 1: 5–11

Miss Persia Pageant

Esther won the Miss Persia Pageant,
a truly spectacular event;
it wasn't her swimsuit
or her answers astute,
Xerxes enjoyed her bedroom talent.

Esther 2

First and Second Maccabees

A Non-Violent Sabbath Can't Be Passive

"We are concerned for virtue and right;
because it's the Sabbath we won't fight.
Though you are militant
we will die innocent."
A thousand were slaughtered by that night.

1 Maccabees 2: 29—38

Prayers for the Dead

Here's a topic that we might discuss:
Judas thought it not superfluous
'cause of resurrection
(then a new conception)
to make off'rings for the dead 'mong us.

Second Maccabees 12: 43—46

Job

Job's Wife

Old Job of Uz was a patient guy
who suffered much, but never knew why,
lost cattle and children,
then his wife said to him,
"Job, why don't you curse God and die?"

Job 2:9

Who Was the Shortest Man in the Bible?

It's a feud that's caused more heat than light,
answer the question, try if you might:
Who was the shortest man
in the biblical plan?
I think it was Bildad the Shuhite.

Job 2: 11

Shoe height. . . Get it? He was short. . . Groan.

After this Job Opened his Mouth and Cursed the Day

Woe! For it's just as I've always feared,
that which I have held in dread is here;
there's no peace, no quiet,

I live with disquiet
for my life by turmoil is smeared.

Job 3: 25–26

Eliphaz Speaks

A word to me was secretly brought,
by my ears was this slight whisper caught;
it caused me to tremble,
my bones disassemble;
by a ghost was I this message taught.

Can a mortal be purer than God?
It is extraordinarily odd
to think yourself noble
in your plight ignoble;
you should by the Lord be overawed.

Job 4: 12–17

My Days Are Few

My days are few, oh God, so desist;
leave me alone, I cannot resist.
I'll go down to that gloom
which is my aphotic doom;
let me be and I'll cease to exist.

Job 10: 20–22

Male Nipples

I really don't want to raise quibbles,
but this verse is bound to cause ripples
of laughter as it's read.

Sure, Job, go right ahead,
just try to get milk from male nipples.

Job 21:24 (KJV)

And though I joke, galactorrhea, or male lactation, does occur
occasionally.

Behemoth!

Job, the Behemoth should be your sign
to indicate how power's defined.
Just one glance divulges
with vigor he bulges;
his penis stiffens just like the pine.

Job 40:17

Read this verse in the translations by Robert Alter and Stephen
Mitchel.

My Behemoth

Who is it that can make the sea wroth?
And who comes up from the bubbling froth?
You follow where he goes
and try to pierce his nose,
but you'll never catch my Behemoth!

Job 40: 23–24

Psalms

No Bankers

Who can find a home in Yahweh's tent?
Who to his mountain can make ascent?
Not bankers, 'parently,
for they do willingly
loan cash and charge interest on it.

Psalm 15: 1–5

Interesting

"Scripture is good," he loudly intones,
except this one, this one he'll disown,
"for our economy
is structured so, you see,
that we must charge interest on loans."

Psalm 15: 5

A Feast before My Enemies

Yahweh's my shepherd; I won't despair.
He lays me a feast in my foes' lair,
but is that to shame them,
to debase and condemn,
or will I be expected to share?

Psalm 23: 5

Psalm 24 in a Capitalist Economy

The earth is the LORD's–from sky to seas,
the soil, the land, the grass and trees,
all except what is owned,
and for profit rezoned
by multinational companies.

Psalm 24:1

Alternative Facts Won't Cut It

Who to the Lord's hill can aspire?
Who shall ascend and then go higher?
Those of clean heart and hand,
but forever God-banned
is the man whose pants are on fire.

Psalm 24: 3–4

Putrescence

I said nary a word, but my groans
broke the silence along with my moans;
day and night was God's hand
heavy upon me and
putrescence was made of my bones.

Psalm 32: 3–4

God, Just Stop Looking at Me!

Lord, listen to my prayer and sad cry;
do not ignore my weeping and sighs.
I'm a stranger to thee,

now look away from me,
so I can rejoice before I die.

Psalm 39: 12–13

Allahu Akbar!

On Zion, which is in the north far,
the musical sons of Korah are
singing a psalm of praise,
and they're chanting the phrase:
"Great is the Lord"–*Allahu Akbar!*

Psalm 48: 1–2

King David Was Wrong

King David admits his guilt, it's true,
but adds, "God I've sinned 'gainst only you."
I won't say he's a liar,
but what of Uriah?
He should start his confession anew.

Psalm 51:4

Frenemy

It's not the hate of my enemy
that causes me the worst injury,
that I could lightly bear,
but I'm caught unaware
by scorn from one who was friend to me.

Psalm 55: 12–14

Even in Iowa?

Can you hear my prayer and cry, oh Yah?
I'm worn out and tired; I'm so raw.
From the ends of the earth
I pray for all I'm worth.
Can you hear me, even in Iowa?

Psalm 61: 1–2

Well That Escalated Quickly

A Psalm of David we now tell:
I thirst for my God in a dry spell.
As for my enemy
who would lie about me,
may he die by sword and go to hell!

Psalm 63

Prey for the Jackal

Those who want me destroyed cackle
thinking of me in death's cold shackle,
but they'll go to the grave
and there nothing will save
them from being prey for the jackal.

Psalm 63: 9–10

Help! Help! I'm Being Repressed!

What we need is a fair arbiter,
someone honest, and wise, and smarter,
who can divide the real

servant burning with zeal
from the jerk who's playing at martyr

Psalm 69: 9

Big-Government Charity

Some of the people on the right wing
say that charity's a private thing,
that protecting the poor
is a personal chore,
but the psalm says it's the work of the king.

Psalm 72

Creation's Cosmic Battle

In the beginning was a titan
twisting in the sea like a python,
till Elohim did crush,
in that primeval hush,
the many heads of Leviathan.

Psalm 74: 14

Peace and Righteousness are Well Met

Salvation's close, not something to miss,
God glories in a land such as this.
Where love and faithfulness
can meet without distress,
peace and righteousness each other kiss.

Psalm 85: 9–10

Praying the Psalms against the President

Still it does dishearten and amaze
to meet someone who frequently prays
with curses to torment
our current president:
"Let him have only a few short days.

Let his progeny be fatherless,
and let no one treat them with largess;
his wife is a bimbo,
Lord, make her a widow."
Is this how we're to show love? I guess. . .

Psalm 109:8–12

He Does What He Wants

Maybe he is baking fresh croissants,
or he's making a list of cool fonts,
or drinking espresso,
but devout psalmists know
God's in heaven; he does what he wants.

Psalm 115: 3

It Just Goes On and On and On. . .

Sometimes reading scripture is a chore;
there are chapters I'd like to ignore,
and if forced to come clean
about Psalm one-nineteen:
frankly, I think that it's a great bore.

Psalm 119

The Contempt of the Proud

Have mercy, oh Lord, and goodwill,
for our souls have had more than their fill
of contempt and of scorn
from those who have not borne
the pains and griefs of life that can kill.

Psalm 123: 3–4

Worst Psalm Ever

The Psalms are lovely, nothing to mock,
but some of them can come as a shock,
and it must be agreed
that it is hard to read
a blessing for smashing babies on rocks.

Psalm 137

King David was Loathsome

Look at me God, and see how I hate;
see how my anger will not abate.
You can examine me;
test my heart, you will see
how loathsome is my natural state.

Psalm 139: 21–23

Teaching to War

The psalmist sings praise to Yahweh for
teaching his hands to battle and war,
but I cannot repeat

this prayer, it is not meet
for me, as violence I abhor.

Psalm 144: 1

Proverbs

Why Is this not Part of our Christian American Tradition?

Can you hear that amazing silence
when we read the biblical guidance:
"Do not envy those who
are violent, and you
should not choose to use their violence."

Proverbs 3: 31

Proverbial Euphemisms

Live all your life with joy and with zest;
enjoy your wife and fondle her breast.
And drink deep from her well,
that's where pleasure will swell,
and may your, *ahem,* 'fountain' be blessed.

Proverbs 5: 15–19

Let Them Satisfy You

So rejoice in the wife of your youth;
let her breasts always satisfy you.
Let them bring you delight
each day and every night–
and I do, yes, oh God! Yes I do!

Proverbs 5: 18–19

A Rigged Game

It is a rigged game–you're bound to lose;
there's no dirty trick they will not use
for the internet troll,
he knows just how to roll:
correct a scoffer and win much abuse.

Proverbs 9: 7

Liars

Those who are honest will rise higher,
be praised in song by heaven's choir,
but there's nothing but woe
for deceivers, you know,
the Lord hates the lips of a liar.

Proverbs 12:22

That's a Bit of a Downer

Even in laughter, the heart sorrows,
and that mirth is mirth that it borrows
for the day speeds away
and the darkness will stay;
there's heaviness for all tomorrows.

Proverbs 14:13

Can't We Just Forget about that Verse?

It's a verse that many would ignore:
He who oppresses the weak and poor,
no matter his station

in this or that nation,
shows much contempt for the Creator.

Proverbs 14:31

It's Not Right

It may be a proverbial rule
that luxury's not fit for a fool,
but just look all around
and see the well-dressed clowns
who don't have the brains God gave a mule.

Proverbs 19: 10

Stay Awake

Solomon said, "Sleep and you'll grow poor;
stay awake and you'll increase your store."
I took a caffeine pill;
twelve days later I'm still
awake, but I can't go on much more.

Proverbs 20: 13

A Proverb that Will Be Forgotten as We React to ISIL

Even if they're cruel as the devil
we shouldn't sink down to their level;
we'll suffer their attack
and we will not strike back.
Do not say, "I will repay evil."

Proverbs 20: 22

Solomon Probably Knew a Thing or two about Quarrelsome Wives

Hear my words if you want a good life;
heed them to avoid unpleasant strife:
Better to be aloof
sitting up on the roof
than share house with a quarrelsome wife.

Proverbs 21: 9

Is it NEE-ther or NEYE-ther?

The author of Proverbs makes a claim:
Preferable to great wealth is fame,
but since I have neither,
I'll just take a breather
and go on as I was, just the same.

Proverbs 22: 1

Some Things Never Change

It seems that some don't care anymore
but it's a fact you cannot ignore,
though it fills us with rue
the old proverb is true:
the rich always rule over the poor.

Proverbs 22: 7

Egyptian Proverbs

There's no need to sulk or be mopey;
accept it, and don't be dopey.
These proverbs were written

in a book Egyptian:
The Wisdom of Amenemope.

Proverbs 22: 17–24: 22

The thirty sayings in this section of Proverbs bear remarkable similarities to the earlier Egyptian book of wisdom instruction, *The Wisdom of Amenemope.* Either the biblical author used the Egyptian book as his source or both authors drew from an even earlier common material.[1]

A Limerick Prayer

Oh, my faith, like my life, is broken;
my hope is not more than a token.
I know I can't fix it,
except *Deus Dixit.*
God, give me a word fitly spoken.

Proverbs 25: 11

That's Treason!

Our objection to this verse is strong;
it most certainly does not belong.
We would rather it said
that we should shoot him dead;
giving aid to the enemy's wrong!

Proverbs 25: 21

The Proper Tool

Give my excellent advice a pass
and you will receive nothing but sass:

1 Crenshaw, *Proverbs,* 516 .

use a rod on the fool,
for that is the proper tool;
beat him just as you would a dumb ass.

Proverbs 26: 3

It's a limerick *and* a pun. . .

I'm So Confused

How can a Christians in faith obey
what the proverbs of Solomon say,
when the first given rule:
"do not answer a fool,"
is trailed by, "answer him the same way."

Proverbs 26: 4–5

Canine Emesis

It cannot be dismissed as a fluke,
no matter how often you rebuke
the fool for his folly
he'll repeat, by golly,
like a dog returning to its puke.

Proverbs 26:11

This One's Usually Ignored

In the list of sins we think rotten
there's one that is often forgotten,
so let's not make excuse
or play fast and play loose.
The Bible also chides the glutton.

Proverbs 28:7

Alternative Facts and Evil Acts

If the leader accepts and then backs
those lies which are "alternative facts,"
be on guard and beware,
you be sure to take care
for his council's up to evil acts.

Proverbs 29: 12

Laws Based On Our Judeo-Christian Values

I'm surprised that we have not heard more
quotes and citations of Proverbs for
guiding our troubled time:
give the poor beer and wine.
Get them drunk so they'll forget they're poor.

Proverbs 31: 6–7

Ecclesiastes

Reverend Killjoy

Preacher Qoheleth might have been wise,
but depression, he couldn't disguise;
he said, "It's all in vain
the same over again;
enjoy it now 'cause everyone dies."

Ecclesiastes 1: 1–2

Worthless!

"Meaningless and vain," says the teacher.
"Worthless!" exclaims the ancient preacher.
"Life's nothing but trouble;
that judgment goes double
for those books where limericks feature.

Ecclesiastes 1: 2

Qoheleth Wouldn't Have a Nice Day

I really do not need an earful
telling me that I should be cheerful,
and get it through your head
that the Preacher has said
it's preferable to be tearful.

Ecclesiastes 7: 3

Rose Colored Memories

I have a suggestion, if you please:
Stop rose coloring your memories.
For it's not very wise
to go on with your sighs;
the old days were not better than these.

Ecclesiastes 7:10

Weapons of War

Here's a verse that we choose to ignore,
if we were asked we could display more,
but this one will suffice,
it is short and concise:
"Wisdom's worth more than weapons of war."

Ecclesiastes 9: 18

Never Mind the Fact that Snakes are Deaf

In the basket a sly serpent sways,
back and forth, as the snake charmer plays,
but if the snake should bite
it's a failure outright,
and the crowd will leave, refusing to pay.

Ecclesiastes 10: 11

The Song of Songs

Laying on of Hands

Here is a scripture that's never bland,
stirring up both my loins and my glands.
I know it can't be wrong
for the Song of all Songs
encourages our "laying on of hands."

Pillow Talk

My lover, your beauty makes me stir,
your breasts are like deer among *les fluers*,
and till the break of day
upon them I will play.
They're the hills of frankincense and myrrh.

Song of Songs 4: 5–6

This is the more discreet reading of "the mountain of myrrh." That
particular slope is more likely to be the fragrant *Mons Pubis*.

A Brief Refractory Period

I have come inside my love's garden,
have gathered my myrrh and spice within;
I have eaten honey

with my lovely bonnie,
and now I'm ready to come again.

Song of Songs 5: 1

King Solomon Was a Randy 'ole Goat

There once was a woman in sandals
whom Solomon liked to handle;
the curve of her smooth thighs
drove the king to loud sighs,
and at her breasts he liked to gambol.

Song of Solomon 7: 1–3

Pudendum

Solomon described her, foot to head
for poetry woos women to bed;
"your navel is refined
may it never lack wine,"
but "navel" isn't what Solomon said.

Our English translations have been tamed
and don't accept what Solomon named,
for we can't even say
the word *vajayjay;*
exposed genitals make us ashamed.

Song of Songs 7: 2

It's a Touchy Subject

While we were together in bed, he
put his left arm under my head, see,
and my love, with his right,

did caress me all night.
Wake up, lover, I am so ready!

Song of Songs 8: 3–4

Boob Variations

For our dear little sister we moan;
she's not developed breasts of her own.
Her milkshake's yet to bring
boys to the yard with rings.
Till then we'll see they leave her alone.

For our dear little sister we moan;
she's not developed breasts of her own.
In an emergency
we'd pay for surgery,
but she prefers her melons home grown.

For our dear little sister we moan;
she's not developed breasts of her own.
Without any knockers
we must ask the doctors,
"Can we help her with some silicone?"

For our dear little sister we moan;
she's not developed breasts of her own.
One day soon her jubblies
will be size Double Ds
until then this is a jug free zone.

Song of Solomon 8: 8

The Book of Wisdom

Creator of Almost Everything

On this I am in no way lying,
though to the creeds I'd be complying:
God made all that has breath,
true, but what about death?
God created all things but dying.

The Wisdom of Solomon 1: 13

Sirach

We Don't Read the Apocrypha, Anyway

The book of Ecclesiasticus
doesn't apply to Protestant us,
so when it says that sin
can be, by almsgivin',
redressed, we ignore it without fuss.

Sirach 3: 30

The apocryphal (or deuterocanonical) book of Sirach is also
known as the Wisdom of Ben Sira or the Book of Sirach (or Sirach
for short) or Ecclesiasticus or even the Wisdom of Jesus son of
Sirach.[1]

Ben Sira Doesn't Trust Divas

My son, I warn you to be wary;
with the singing girl do not tarry,
for this I will predict
you'll be caught by her trick;
her wiles will leave you unmerry.

Sirach 9: 4

---

1. Di Lella, *Wisdom of Ben-Sira,* 932

King Today, Gone Tomorrow

A long illness down in the marrow,
an illness of pain and great sorrow
baffles the physician
with his healing mission;
a king today's a corpse tomorrow.

Sirach 10: 10

The Nothingness of a Man

What is a man, and why should he boast?
He lives for one hundred years, at most;
like droplets in the sea,
lost in eternity.
Without the Lord's mercy he is toast.

Sirach 18: 8–11

I Am Wisdom

I sprang from the mouth of the Most High,
covered the Earth like a mist did I;
alone I ringed heaven
plumbed the abyss even;
I am Wisdom, to me now draw nigh.

Sirach 24

Testicular Trauma

When the humble man or woman calls,
God comes without halts, pauses, or stalls;
he will not be delayed

to see evil repaid
and kick the merciless in the balls.

Sirach 35: 17–20

The Moon

The moon, ever punctual to shine,
to mark the times, everlasting sign;
she waxes in phases
and in the sky raises
the banner of hosts as heaven's shrine.

Sirach 43: 6–8

Isaiah

I Don't Care

I hate all that I am witnessing;
your blood covered hands are glistening.
You may multiply prayer
but I really don't care.
Pray all you want; I'm not listening.

Isaiah 1: 14–15

Assassins and Harlots

See her dressed in robes of rich scarlet,
once full of justice; she's a varlet.
The city of Zion's
become an assassin,
the faithful city, now a harlot.

Isaiah 1:21

You Forgot To Mention the Scabs

The Daughters of Zion are haughty;
they are proud and they have been naughty.
God will wound their vain hearts,
expose their lady parts,
and they'll smell like a porta-potty.

Isaiah 3: 16–24

Something Something Something

In the book of Isaiah we've read,
"The Lord will do something to their head
and to their wherever,"
but really we've never
understood what the old prophet said.

Isaiah 3: 17

Isaiah 3: 17 is a difficult verse to translate properly. It is loaded infrequently used words. "An honest reading admitting our ignorance would render the verse as "The Lord will do something to the tops of the heads of the daughters of Zion and The Lord will do something else to their somethings."[1]

The Daughters of Zion Were Dedicated Followers of Fashion

Daughters of Zion in high fashions
dressed in hoods and veils of fine linens;
they were socialite fools
and wore rings, and nose jewels,
mantles, and wimples, and crisping pins.

Isaiah 3: 18–22 (KJV)

Euphemistically Speaking, that Is. . .

The Seraphs in heaven are beings
created with six wonderful wings:
two to cover their face,
two for flying in space,
and two to cover their private things.

Isaiah 6: 2

1. Gilad, "Isaiah Gave Hebrew,"

"Feet" are often used in the Hebrew Bible as a euphemism for genitals. See also the limerick for Ruth 3: 6–8.

Tiglath-Pileser the Barber

King Ahaz, you must watch and beware:
Assyria's king soon will be there.
That crazy hell raiser
will come with his razor
to shave off your beard and pubic hair.

Isaiah 7: 20

Just as "feet" are often used in the Bible as a euphemism for genitals, here too "hair of the feet" must be understood as polite reference a more shameful shaving.

That's Quite a Moniker, Son

Isaiah's son's name had real pizzazz;
it sounded a bit like modern jazz,
for the name was received
before he was conceived.
He was called Maher-shalal-hash-baz.

Isaiah 8: 1–3

It's not about Satan

No, no. In this you're quite mistaken.
Your interpretation needs straightened,
so hear what I tell ya'
the book of Isaiah
chapter fourteen's not about Satan.

Isaiah 14: 4

Buttocks Exposed

The prophet Isaiah once proposed
to prophesy completely unclothed;
three years the prophet went,
as a sign and portent,
naked and barefoot, buttocks exposed.

Isaiah 20: 2–3

Another Messiah?

Though I risk being called pariah,
or crank, or heretic, or liar,
I would like to point out,
look yourself if you doubt,
Cyrus is another messiah.

Isaiah 45: 1

Cyrus is described as the "anointed one"—the Hebrew word
"messiah."

Good and Evil

Yahweh forms both the dark and the light,
separating the day from the night;
he also creates good,
and when he's in the mood,
makes evil too. Yes, you read that right.

Isaiah 45: 7

Bill O'Reilly Reacts to Isaiah 55

God, you know that I am most devout,
but you're giving people a handout!

Buy food without money?
Giving it away free?
You and I have things we must sort out!

Isaiah 55: 1

Filthy Rags

Craig loves his Bible, but his faith lags;
a part of him recoils and he gags
when Isaiah tells us
that all our righteousness
is like discarded menstrual rags.

Isaiah 64:6

Jeremiah

One or the Other, Jeremiah

Ole' Jeremiah was quite clever,
his prophecies are great, however
there's a discrepancy
that is bothering me:
Is or is not God's wrath forever?

Jeremiah 3:12, 17: 4

The Prophet's Rejection Letter

Jeremiah, your writing, I fear,
is just too dark to be published here:
in depression drifting
your words aren't uplifting,
and what's with the "uncircumcised ear"?

Jeremiah 6:10

It's not the Christmas Tree

Despite the claims of an absurd few
that the prophet demands we eschew
our decorated trees
in these festivities,
he damns idols, not the Christmas yew.

Jeremiah 10: 2–4

The Men of Anathoth

I was like a trusting, slaughtered lamb,
misled by those with an evil plan.
"Let's destroy him," they said.
"Let's make sure that he's dead."
Yahweh, let your vengeance on them slam.

Jeremiah 11: 18–20

Immediate Redress

Righteous Yahweh, oh why do you bless
those who are continu'lly faithless?
You plant them, they take root,
they grow and e'en bear fruit;
Lord, this needs immediate redress.

Jeremiah 12: 1–3

Woe to Me and My Mother

Oh mother! Why did you give me birth,
a man of dispute to the whole earth?
I don't lend or borrow,
but to my great sorrow
they will curse me for all that they're worth.

Jeremiah 15: 10

A Deceptive Stream

God! Yahweh, you make me want to scream.
I am wounded for preaching your theme;
I'm led to the slaughter.

Like uncertain water,
you are, to me, a deceptive stream.

Jeremiah 15: 18

Yahweh Responds to Jeremiah's Complaint

Thus says Yahweh: "I know that you're spent
but if you will shut up and repent,
I will let you return,
but to them you can't turn;
let your speech to truth, not trash, be bent."

Jeremiah 15: 19

The Partridge and the Capitalist

The partridge is a bird who will raid
bird nests to hatch eggs it has not laid,
exactly like the jerk
who gets rich without work;
Oh Lord, let them all as fools be paid.

Jeremiah 17:11

Not You Too, God

You, Yahweh, have made me the bearer
of bad news to those who're in error.
They hate and despise me,
so now, please, don't you be
another source of shock and terror.

Jeremiah 17:17

Jeremiah Takes it all Back

Remember, God, how I prayed for them,
I stood before you, spoke good of them?
Well, alas and alack!
Now I take it all back:
to death them and their children condemn!

Jeremiah 18: 20–21

Jeremiah's Lament

You seduced me and I was deceived,
the words I speak have not been received;
if I'm silent, I burn,
if I speak I am spurned.
Can you wonder that I am aggrieved?

Jeremiah 20: 7–9

Why Curse Him?

Jeremiah, I understand why
the sound of your curses fills the sky,
but tell me why you damn
the comradely old man
with news of your birth; why should he die?

Jeremiah 20: 15–17

The Burial of an Ass

The prophet rebuked Jehoiakim,
with strong words he was fiercely condemned,
no lament for him be heard.

This king won't be interred.
Drag that ass out of Jerusalem.

Jeremiah 22: 18–19

Jeremiah Was Wrong

Jeremiah cursed Jehoiakim,
said, "He'll have no sons to follow him."
But the prophet was wrong;
though his rule wasn't long,
the next king was prince Jehoiachin.

Jeremiah 36:30, 2 Kings 24: 6, 8

Lamentations

Unsavory

Here I am, the man unsavory,
under the rod of the Lord's fury.
He's led me, day and night,
into darkness, not light.
I'm wasted and broken and dreary.

Lamentations 3: 1–4

Any Translation with Sea Monsters in It
Is a Good Translation

I suppose it is time I confessed—
seldom do I like KJV best,
but how could I resist
a supernat'ral twist:
"even sea monsters draw out the breast. . ."

Lamentations 4:3 (KJV)

Baruch

Amanuensis

Don't think of it as gratuitous;
that we have it is fortuitous,
and don't neglect this book
for forgotten Baruch
was Jeremiah's amanuensis.

Baruch 1–6

Ezekiel

Giorgio A. Tsoukalos Has an Explanation for Everything

I love the History Channel show
claiming Ezekiel couldn't know
that what heaven reveals
in those wheels within wheels
was actually a U.F.O.

Ezekiel 1: 4–12

Ezekiel Eats the Scroll

Then the voice said, "I want you to eat
this scroll, so don't you make me repeat."
It tasted like honey
but made me feel funny;
the word for Israel was bitter-sweet.

Ezekiel 3: 1–15

Diagnosed with Schizophrenia

With his bouts of catatonia,
and his bizarre neurasthenia,
though it might cause chagrin,
perhaps he should have been
diagnosed with schizophrenia.

Ezekiel 4: 4–6

God's Own Recipe

Now, Ezekiel, don't pitch a fit,
here's some bread, I want you to eat it;
it's my own recipe
for health and remedy.
Don't freak out—it was baked over shit.

Ezekiel 4: 9–12

No Excuse

"The Limerick," she said, "is, of course,
far too vulgar and overly coarse
for a prophet to use,
and there is no excuse
for Ezek'el to mention the horse."

Ezekiel 23

There Is No Appreciation for this Verse

There is a biblical citation
that receives no appreciation:
it's all gross spectacles
of donkey genitals
and of horses' ejaculations!

Ezekiel 23: 20

The Prophet's Art Gets Some Folks Excited

There were two girls, allegorical,
part of Ezekiel's oracle.
Their bosoms were caressed

and their nipples were pressed. . .
Relax! It's merely rhetorical.

Ezekiel 23: 2–3

Ezekiel's Failed Prediction

What Ezekiel said of Tyre
never did completely transpire;
King Nebuchadnezzar
came as the aggressor,
but stopped the siege when he did tire.

Ezekiel 26

Nebuchadnezzar laid siege to the city of Tyre for 13 years (ca. 585–573), but failed to completely reduce the city to rubble as the prophet predicted.[1] Ezekiel seems to acknowledge his error a few chapters later when he prophecies that Nebuchadnezzar will rub his head bald in trying to subdue the city, but will derive no profit for himself or his army (Ezekiel 29: 18).

Vale of Bones

Now the prophet was educated
in the Vale of Bones Desiccated,
where the bones assembled
and in the wind trembled
until they were resuscitated.

Ezekiel 37

1. Katzenstein, H. J. "Tyre," 690.

Daniel

The Daniel Diet

No, the Bible did not supply it;
ignore those who want you to buy it.
They that published the books
are little more than crooks,
peddling a baseless Daniel Diet.

Daniel 1: 8–18

Daniel's Apocalyptic Menagerie

First was a lion plucked of its wings,
then came a bear told, "Eat many things!"
Third, a leopard to dread
with wings and four strange heads;
last was a beast with horns that were kings.

Daniel 7

They Had some Nervy

Susanna was a woman curvy;
she was spied upon by two pervy
elders who were unjust
and inflamed with much lust.
They wanted sex. They had some nervy!

Daniel 13: 1–21

Bel and the Dragon

Said the king, "Bel lives! See how he eats?"
Said Daniel, "He's not, not in the least."
When the trick was exposed,
the hidden door was closed
and the king killed all Bel's lying priests.

They also worshipped a giant snake,
said the king, "You can't claim this one's fake."
But without sword or stick
Daniel killed it, no trick.
He fed it tar: death by belly ache.

Daniel 14: 1–27

Hosea

This One's a Doozy

Hosea, listen, don't get woozy.
I want you to marry a floozy,
that's right, and what is more,
have children with the whore;
I told you this task was a doozy.

Hosea 1: 2

Misogynist

Without saying he should be dismissed,
I think that we really should insist
Hosea the prophet
was, at least just a bit,
something of a cruel misogynist.

Hosea 2: 1–13

To be fair however, the shocking threats of violent revenge and death in the first half of chapter two give way in the second half to the prophet's hope for reconciliation with his wayward wife.[1]

---

1. Weems, *Battered Love*, 92- 93

Joel

It's not the DT's Causing this Vision

Wake up, you drunkards, it's time to weep;
there's no more wine to put you to sleep.
Now direct your focus
to the horde of locusts
that soon over all Israel will sweep.

Joel 1: 4–5

Bloodmoon Hullabaloo

The Dispensationalist, he mines
Joel's description of heavenly signs
with each lunar eclipse;
then he rewrites his scripts
and his predictions he redefines.

Joel 2: 30–32

Amos

Eschatological Expectations

Our enemies will be in distress
on the great day of Yahweh, oh yes!
"Oh no!" says the prophet,
"that day *you* will regret
'cause you fail the poor in your praxis."

Amos 5: 11–18

Go Home and Pluck Your Figs

Said Amaziah to Amos, "You prig!
We don't want prophecies here. You dig?
You're noxious in Bethel;
stick around, you'll catch hell.
Why don't you go home and pluck your figs?"

Amos 7: 10–13

I Am not a Prophet

"I am not a prophet," said Amos,
"nor is my father someone famous;
I am just a shepherd,
a man who heard the word,
but Israel, you're an ignoramus."

Amos 7: 14–17

Obadiah

It's Only 21 Verses

Some of the prophets will bring us grief,
and some of them speak of sweet relief,
but it would be a sin
to neglect the vision
of Obadiah, however brief.

Obadiah 1: 1–21

Jonah

Not too many words rhyme with Jonah

There once was a prophet named Jonah
who thought that from God he could run-ah;
he was caught by a fish
when death was his one wish
and forced to bring hope to Nineveh.

Jonah 1: 1–4: 11

Fish Gastric Juices

Your literal reading produces
many interpretive abuses,
but still you will contrive
to show Jonah survive
three full days in fish gastric juices.

Jonah 1: 17

Micah

A Word for the Cannibals

You consume the flesh of my people,
stripping their bones, Oh! You are evil.
So you'll cry out to God,
but he won't even nod;
you'll be alone in this upheaval.

Micah 3: 3–4

Micah Flubbed

The prophet Micah pronounced his call:
"Assyria's coming to waste us all;
Zion will be rubble!"
But to burst your bubble:
he flubbed, Jerusalem didn't fall.

Micah 3: 12

Micah's prophecy of Jerusalem's destruction during the reign of King Hezekiah did not come to pass. Was this a failure of prophecy? Should Micah be labeled as a false prophet? Or did his message of impending doom so impact his audience that their repentance moved Yahweh to relent? That seems to be the interpretation of the later prophet Jeremiah, who reminded the people of his age of Micah's words (Jeremiah 26: 18–19). "Yet, Jerusalem, in spite of a history of conflicts that continue to our day, has never been reduced to a plowed field or a hill 'overgrown with thickets' (v.12 NIV). Since biblical times, there has always been a city there."[1]

1. Simundson, Daniel J. "Micah"560.

Nahum

City of Blood

"Woe to the lying city of blood!"
said Nahum, that and some other crud.
He was shot through with hate
which came out in a spate
of raging bitterness like a flood.

Nahum 3: 1

Nahum's Woe to Nineveh

God said to Nin'veh, "You're a disgrace;
I'll lift your skirts up over your face.
I will pelt you with shit
till you are sick of it;
but don't expect comfort in this place."

Nahum 3: 5–7

Habakkuk

Are You There God? It's Me, Habakkuk

Habakkuk complained to God on high,
"How long must 'Violence!' be my cry?
The law is paralyzed,
strife abounds, justice dies,
and I'm not convinced you hear me sigh."

Habakkuk 1: 1–4

The Horned God

Parts of scripture are poetic, and
I believe that is really quite grand,
but it's hard to conceive
and harder to believe
that God has horns coming from his hands.

Habakkuk 3: 4 (KJV)

Zephaniah

Creation Reversed

I will sweep away the humans first,
then creatures, and birds, and fish submersed.
I'll topple the fiendish
for all their uncleanness;
I will see my creation reversed.

Zephaniah 1: 2–3

Zephaniah's Complaint

Jerusalem's prophets are reckless,
so irresponsible and feckless;
the priests are all profane,
from justice they abstain.
Jerusalem is far from speckless.

Zephaniah 3: 1–4

Haggai

Haggai Who?

The book of Haggai seems to fly by;
it's lost between Zeph and Zechari—
and even when it's found
devout readers are bound
to ask the question, "who was that guy?"

Zechariah

With Dream Sequences by Salvador Dali

I dreamt of a girl in a basket
and so I asked, "What is this mascot?"
Then there were more strange things,
two women with stork wings
who bore it away like a casket.

Zechariah 5: 5–11

To the Worthless Shepherd

Woe, and woe to the worthless shepherd,
you who would leave your flock, hear this word:
because you've gone awry,
to gouge out your right eye,
and slash your right arm, I'll send a sword!

Zechariah 11: 17

Malachi

Esau Got a Bad Rap

I am not sure why it is stated
that to Jacob God's love was slated;
he was a trickster thief,
and it strains our belief
that it was Esau that God hated.

Malachi 1: 2–3

Shitfaced

Listen priests, you've become a disgrace;
behave or I'll put you in your place.
Your blessings I will curse
and then I'll make it worse,
I will smear dung all over your face.

Malachi 2: 1–3

Matthew

The Father Pretend

Explain to me why does Matthew end
his genealogy with Joseph, when
it is quite obvious,
to the sharp audience,
that he's only the father pretend?

Matthew 1: 1–25

No Virgins There

"Behold a virgin shall bear a son,"
that verse is in Matthew chapter one;
he's quoting the prophet
Isaiah, of old, but
of virgins in that text, there are none.

Matthew 1: 23, Isaiah 7:14

The quotation is given from the Septuagint (LXX) translation which changed the Hebrew *'almah* "young woman" to the Greek word *parthenos* which means "virgin." Matthew ignores the historical context of the quotation and makes of it a promise for the future, understanding it as a prophecy of Jesus' birth.[1]

1. Hooker, *Beginnings,* 32

Which Prophet Was He Quoting?

The critics are often found gloating
over the error in Matthew, noting
that the prophets sayeth
he'd be from Nazareth;
they ask, "Which prophet was he quoting?"

Matthew 2: 23

Though Matthew cites "the prophets" you will find no reference
to the Messiah coming from Nazareth, and "no single prophecy
exists which says that the Messiah was to be called a Nazarene."[2]

They Can Have what's Left

From Indianapolis to Perth
the meek aren't given what they are worth,
but we've gone 'round the bend,
and soon our wars will end,
then they can have what's left of the earth.

Matthew 5: 5

Secret. Not Secret

Jesus, you first said, 'let them be seen,'
and then, with little space in between,
you told us that we need
to keep any good deed
secret–now, tell us, which do you mean?

Matthew 5: 16, 6: 1

2. Robertson, *Word Pictures*, 21

Capitalist Fool

Jesus said to call no one a fool
and we follow this general rule
applied to everyone
with one small exception
for the wealthy capitalist tool.

Matthew 5: 22, Luke 12: 20

Modern Christians Respond

That Jesus guy's an absolute fool;
his instruction's totally uncool.
He says, 'do not strike back
when you're under attack.'
We don't believe we're bound to this rule.

Matthew 5: 38–39

In "God" We Trust

Here is something we should examine
whether we're 'Merican or Roman:
it is frustrating and odd
that we can't worship God
while given in service to Mammon.

Matthew 6: 24 (KJV)

You Who Are Evil Know How To Give Good Gifts

If your son requests a piece of bread,
would you give the boy a stone instead?
If he asks you for fish,

would you crush the boy's wish
and give him a snake? Is your brain dead?

Matthew 7: 9–10

Jesus Committed Treason

Healing the slave of the Centur'on,
no matter the cause or the reason,
gave comfort and aid to
the enemy, and you
must treat it as an act of treason.

Matthew 8: 5–13

Bill O'Reilly Reacts to the Feeding of the Five Thousand

Bill was there with Jesus by the sea;
he watched Jesus give away food–free!
Said Bill, "It should be clear
what you're creating here
is a culture of dependency."

Matthew 14: 13–21

Origen Took It Very Seriously, Indeed

Origen said, "My Jesus enthralls;
I will accept his ascetic calls."
With a knife serrated
he himself castrated:
received the gospel and lost his balls.
Matthew 19: 12

The early Church father, Origen Adamantius voluntarily lived a
life of extreme asceticism, going so far, it is reported, as to take
Jesus' words about those who have made themselves "eunuchs for

the kingdom" literally and castrated himself. [3] Though there is
some question as to whether or not this really happened.

We Mostly Demur

Said Jesus, who is our great mentor,
"It is hard for the rich to enter
into God's Kingdom, true,
like pushing camels through
needles' eyes." But we mostly demur.

Matthew 19: 23–24

World Champion Trick Rider

It would appear in reading's first pass
that in Jerusalem's crowded mass,
to meet the prophet's text,
though it leaves us perplexed,
he straddled both the foal and the ass.

Matthew 21: 7

Straining Camels

Down went a camel and tiger-cat,
a hippo, and a vampire bat,
but the filter in place
prevented a disgrace.
So glad I didn't swallow the gnat!

Matthew 23: 24

---

3. Gonzáles, *Story of Christianity,* 137

The Abomination of Desolation

When you see the Abomination
set up in the sacred location,
if you're in Judea
you will have to flee-a;
make an immediate migration.

Matthew 24: 15–18

Which Way Did He Go?

Now I am confused and full of doubt,
which of the accounts should I give clout?
Was it as Matt. described,
his death was suicide,
or did he fall and his guts gush out?

Matthew 27:5. Acts 1:18

Mark

Preexistence

There's been much debate and insistence,
persistence and reasoned resistance.
It could lead to dismay,
but what does Mark's book say
about Jesus' preexistence?

Mark 1:1

John the Baptizer

John the Baptizer's one to beware;
going about in his underwear,
leather belt at his waist,
he never feels disgraced
though his clothes are made of camel hair.

Mark 1: 6

Pity or Indignation?

A leper came to Christ's location
to be cured of his degradation;
Jesus said, "I'm willing,"
but was he feeling
pity or was it indignation?

Mark 1: 40–41

Most of the Greek manuscripts of the New Testament say that Jesus was moved "with compassion," for the man, however a few read "Jesus became angered" or "indignant."[1]

My Roof's Broke

The man of house where Jesus spoke
saw men on his roof a large hole poke,
digging with axe and a pick
to drop the par'lytic.
"That's great," he said, "but now my roof's broke!"

Mark 2: 1–12

Parable of the Growing Seed

So the Kingdom of God is like this:
a man scatters his seeds, hit or miss,
then, while he is sleeping,
grain grows up for reaping,
but he takes no credit for all this.

Mark 4: 26–29

He Did not Speak to Them without a Parable

When the great crowds of people draw near
Jesus speaks in a way they can hear:
he speaks in parable
to make it bearable,
but his disciples need it made clear.

Mark 4:34

1. Mann, *Mark*, 219

Jesus the Prestidigitator

We will have to answer the question:
was Jesus, in fact, a magician?
With symbolic gesture
he effected the cure,
a spit / magic word combination.

Mark 7:31–34

Spitting on the Blind

Jesus was a healer sent by God,
though his method was just a bit odd.
Would it be a surprise
that to heal blind men's eyes
Jesus, on them, would spit phlegmy wads?

Mark 8: 22–23

Hold the Salt, Please

Some verses cause me to perspire,
for they sound so awfully dire;
sometimes Jesus is dark.
Take this statement in Mark,
"Everyone will be salted with fire!"

Mark 9:49

Anti-Miracle Crowds

Jesus, going the Jericho route,
did anti-miracle crowds refute;
when the blind man spoke loud

the antagonist crowd
tried to make poor Bartimaeus mute.

Mark 10: 46–52

Cursing the Fig Tree

Now leaving Bethany in the east,
our Jesus was hungry for a feast,
saw a fig tree *en route*,
oh, but it had no fruit,
so upon it a curse he released.

Mark 11: 12

Beware

Beware the teacher who espouses
the law and walks out in fine blouses;
they who make lengthy prayers
are just putting on airs
and they devour poor widows' houses.

Mark 12: 38–39

A Votive for Judas

I know it's just not done, but what if
for old Judas, we lit a votive?
Yes, he betrayed Jesus,
and that rightly grieves us,
but we don't know Judas' motive.

Mark 14: 10

The Naked Fugitive

One disciple managed to elude
the guards taking Jesus to the rood.
They grabbed at his linen,
he twisted, went spinnin',
slipped from his clothes and ran away nude.

Mark 14: 51–52

Well, That Was Unexpected

Of Jesus I am a devotee,
but I think that we can all agree
what, with the dejection
and no resurrection,
Mark's gospel ends rather abruptl. . .

Mark 16: 1–8

Mark's gospel seems to end abruptly mid-sentence at 16:8, and there is no satisfactory explanation for this. An early attempt to fix the problem supplied a longer ending (16: 9–20) but these verses are not found in the most reliable manuscripts of the gospel.[2]

666 Is Mark's Number

Ignore all the threats and the curses,
I know what John's number rehearses:
for the truth you must hark
that the Gospel of Mark
has six hundred sixty-six verses.

Mark 16:8. Revelation 13: 18

This assumes you stop counting at the original ending of Mark's gospel.

2. Grant, "Exegesis," 915

Snake Handlers

If the Bible is perfectly true
we must do all that it says to do
without interpreting,
or critical thinking;
pick up snakes, even if they bite you.

Mark 16: 18

Luke

So Bucolic

Unless we claim it's hyperbolic,
Mary's song is quite vitriolic;
kings are to be pulled down,
the poor raised from the ground. . .
And we thought she was so bucolic!

Luke 1: 46–55

Unconfirmed by History

Luke says Augustus gave a decree
to make a count of everybody
in the Roman Empire,
and though Luke's no liar
this can't be confirmed by history.

Luke 2: 1–3

The only census we know to have been conducted while Quirnius was governor in Syria (as Luke indicates) happened about ten years too late to have been the occasion for the nativity story.[1]

1. Brown, *Birth*, 413

Messiah?

Though Herod thought him a pariah,
the crowds said, 'he's one we admiah,'
all across the nation
they had expectations:
could John the Baptist be Messiah?

Luke 3: 15

Your Future Is Bleak

Blessed are you who are poor and meek;
blessed are you when they call you weak
but woe upon the rich
living without an itch.
You laugh now, but your future is bleak.

Luke 6: 20–26

There Once Was a Gal from Magdala

There once was a gal from Magdala
whose life was anything but gala,
she had seven demons
till Jesus brought reason,
casting them from her amygdala.

Luke 8: 2, Mark 16:9

Missionary Position

Jesus sent his friends on a mission:
"Tell everyone of sin's remission;
when you stay in a home
don't from house to house roam.

That's the missionary's position."

Luke 10: 7

No Wonder We're so Ambivalent about Public Breast Feeding

Did Luke have a literary lapse,
momentarily confused perhaps?
It's not quite distressing
but he wrote of blessing
both the suckled and unsuckled paps.

Luke 11:27, 23:29 in the KJV

Unprofitable

Jesus speaks of the prophet Abel,
but how should he carry this label?
How was the role conferred?
When did he speak God's word?
These questions are unprofitable.

Luke 11: 50–51

Some Men just Want To Watch the World Burn

I've come to set the world on fire;
I wish the flames were burning higher!
I came not to bring peace
but divide, piece by piece.
Doesn't that excite and inspire?

Luke 12: 49–51

Jesus Isn't Very Good at Family Counseling

Do you suppose that I came to be meek?
Not at all, it's division I seek!
This is how it will be:
two will side against three,
setting mothers and daughters to shriek.

Luke 12:51–53

Pontius Pilate

Pontius Pilate wasn't very nice,
he was brutal to be more precise:
he frightened plebeians,
and killed Galileans
then mixed the blood with their sacrifice.

Luke 13:1

Not a Quid Pro Quo

If your faith and devotion you'd show
share a meal with the poor folks you know;
give to the dismembered
but try to remember
charity is not a *quid pro quo*.

Luke 14: 12–14

Hate Family

Now we read from Luke in the Bible
of Jesus, the rabbi archetypal,
who said, "to follow me
you must hate family,

or you cannot be my disciple."

Luke 14:26

Lazarus the Beggar

Lazarus, the beggar, was so poor
that he lay at the gate on the floor
begging for scraps to eat
while the dogs of the street
came and licked pus from his oozing sores.

Luke 16: 20–21

"A Christmas Carol" Is All Wrong

It's clear that Luke's gospel was absent
as Dickens penned his Christmas pageant:
spectral emanations
and ghost visitations
won't be enough to make Scrooge repent.

Luke 16: 31

Black Eye

The judge was an irrev'rent bad guy
to whom the widow came to apply;
she said: "Do what is right!"
and the poor judge took fright,
"If I don't she'll give me a black eye."

Luke 18: 1–7

Zounds!

Jesus, in Luke's parable of the pounds,
makes a statement that really astounds:
"As for my enemies,
slay them here before me!"
"Yikes!" I say, "Gadzooks, and even zounds!"

Luke 19:27

Jesus, Did You Forget?

Jesus, we know you're a teacher deft,
not at all like those loons on the left,
but you thoughtlessly say
we should Caesar's tax pay!
Did you forget: taxation is theft!?

Luke 20: 21–25

Polyandry Is just Ludicrous

The Sadducees come with a question,
one to force Jesus' accession,
but it won't work unless
polyandry is less
believable than resurrection.

Luke 20: 27–38

The Resurrection as a Scatological Event

So here it is: the biblical scoop,
raised up Jesus ate fish with the group.
But I wonder, did he,
in his glor'fied body
after that have to pee and to poop?

Luke 24: 41–43

John

John the Sectarian

I hate to be so contrarian,
but what did you expect, Darian?
With polemic attack
going forward and back,
John's gospel is quite sectarian.

Wrapped Up in Skin

The Word came to us wrapped up in skin,
the fullness of God's glory within;
full of grace, he was true
with his glory in view,
the glory of Father God, even.

John 1:14

Skeptical

Some Christians think it heretical
to express dubiousness at all,
but John's gospel does tell
that good old Nathanael,
the True Israelite, was skeptical.

John 1:45–46

Not in This Army

Once Jesus made wine for everyone
with a Eucharistic overtone,
but, unfortunately,
in William Booth's Army
this text can be a forgotten one.

John 2: 1–11

The Salvation Army is an alcohol-abstaining, non-sacramental denomination.

He Did! No, He Didn't!

Jesus baptized, and did it a lot,
so much that the Pharisees got hot.
We could take this as true,
but wait, according to
John's final redactor he did not.

John 3: 23, 4: 1–2

An Interpolated Angel

When the angel comes the water's stirred;
first one in gets all his ailments cured.
But closer inspection
of this gospel section
shows it's an interpolated word.

John 5:4

Though it may reflect an authentic popular tradition, the reference to the angel is not in the earliest manuscripts of John's gospel.[1]

1. Brown, *John, 207.*

What Did He Write?

"Should we stone her, hit her with a brick?"
They intended the question as a trick,
but Jesus, he knelt down
and he wrote in the ground.
Did he perhaps write a limerick?

John 8: 1–11

This Story's Been Hacked

The woman needs her story unpacked;
if she were caught mid sexual act
there must have been a man
because no woman can
do that alone and that is a fact.

John 8: 3–11

Strange Friendship

Here's friendship of a very strange brand,
a relationship based on demand:
said Jesus at the end
to those he would call friend,
"you're friends if you do what I command."

John 15:14

Dispensationalists Like To Say

Dispensationalists like to say
that Christians will be raptured someday,
but I think they've ignored

the last prayer of our Lord:
"I don't ask you to take them away. . ."

John 17: 15

Make Them One

It's not only for these that I pray
but for all who will believe some day.
Father, please make them one
else my work is undone;
if they clash help them love anyway.

John 17: 20–26

Who's on Trial Here?

Pilate wears an ironic smile
and Jesus responds without guile.
It's not Jesus who fears,
as John's gospel makes clear
it's really Pilate who's on trial

John 19: 9–16

Whose Twin?

Now here is a curiosity:
in the Gospel of John we can see
that Thomas was called "Twin,"
but we're left wonderin'-
should we try to guess? Whose twin was he?

John 20:24

Acts

Beyond Our Apprehension

Still it's beyond our apprehension
just how Jesus made his ascension.
Without saying goodbye
he rose up through the sky,
carried to another dimension.

Acts 1: 9

Akeldama

Judas turned out to be quite a dud;
he was one of us, but no more, bud,
for he took his money
and bought a field where he
fell headlong, spilled intestines and blood.

Acts 1: 16–19

The Kingdom Is Bigger

The African eunuch, he did pause;
he'd have been excluded for his flaws
but Phillip realized
that he should be baptized;
the kingdom is bigger than old laws.

Acts 8: 26–39

You'da Cussed Too!

Now Paul was not a great orator,
to put it plainly–he was a bore;
Eutychus grew sleepy
as Paul droned on, and he
fell from the window on the third floor.

Acts 20: 9

Ironically, *Eutychus* means "fortunate."[1]

That Might Be Taking It out of Context

Management can be filled with dipsticks;
it's as if their heads are stuffed with bricks.
The Bible, it speaks true
when it says unto you:
It is hard to kick against the pricks.

Acts 26:14 (KJV)

Euroclydon

Though the time for sailing was foregone
the Centurion said, "We press on."
To stop, Paul did entreat,
but when we rounded Crete
up came the rough wind, Euroclydon.

Acts 27: 9–14(KJV)

1. Thayer, *Lexicon*, 263.

Loose and Watery with Visible Blood

Some parts of our scripture provoke only yucks,
stories of diseases run amuck;
Publius' father
was sick, his death was sure
till Paul cured him of his bloody flux.

Acts 28:8 (KJV)

Romans

Let Us Exult

Hardships develop perseverance,
suffering builds up our endurance
and that builds character
(which is something quite rare)
this culminates in hope's appearance.

Romans 5: 3–5

Not My President

Paul said, "Obey the authorities,
they've been ordained by God, if you please."
But you will ignore this
and stubbornly insist
this president's from the wrong party!

Romans 13: 1

The Verse Paul Actually Intended

The one who eats meat, eats and enjoys
and in thanking God he makes much noise,
but one who will abstain
makes of himself a pain.
Good God! Vegetarians annoy.

Romans 14: 6

Be Warned

My Bible I have faithfully read;
I like, especially, what Paul said:
Greet each other like this,
with a nice holy kiss,
but be warned, that's how mono gets spread.

Romans 16:16

A Transgendered Apostle

A question infrequently tendered:
How is the name "Junias" rendered?
Chrysostom says female,
while Luther says male.
When was the apostle transgendered?

Romans 16:7

All of the earliest Christian writings referred to Junias as a woman. It wasn't until the medieval period, when small minded copyists, who couldn't imagine a female apostle, changed the name to the masculine Junias.[1]

Tertius Gets his Say

I, Tertius, wrote this epistle
and now I'm trying not to bristle,
'cause I've done all the work,
and Paul, that big ole jerk,
won't let me say much in this missal.

Romans 16: 22

1. Lampe, "Junias," 1127.

First and Second Corinthians

It Means Soft or Pliable

It's an obscure Greek word, *malakos*,
though rare, it's gathered a bit of dross;
quite without precedent
it's made "effeminate"
and the word's real meaning's all but lost.

1 Corinthians 6: 9 (KJV)

The Greek word means "soft, as in soft clothing."[1]

Arsenokoitai

It is hard for the scholar to say
what the apostle meant in his day;
what was to be enjoined
when in writing he coined
that bizarre word *arsenokoitai.*

1 Corinthians 6: 9

Paul seems to have coined this word by combining the Greek
words for "man" and bed"–but his intended meaning is not exactly
clear.

---

1. Thiselton, "Can Hermeneutics," 167.

Eating Food Offered to Idols

Of course it is true that the idols
are not gods and can't be God's rivals,
but there are some who think
that to take food or drink
offered them would be suicidal.

So hear me now, and this is vital,
don't let your freedom break the idyll;
don't swell with arrogance
and wound the weak conscience.
You're free, but let love be your bridle.

1 Corinthians 8: 1–13

Because of the Angels

Paul said weird stuff, but strangest of all:
"Women must always cover their skull,
because of the angels."
Because of the angels?!
What the hell does that even mean, Paul?

1 Corinthians 11: 5–10

Fun House Mirror

I can't make the world any clearer,
all that I try just makes it queerer;
it's all imperfection,
distorted reflection
that we see in a fun house mirror.

1 Corinthians 13: 12

All Means All (Or Maybe It Doesn't)

Why are we certain that "all" means "all"
when we discuss death from Adam's fall,
but we cannot allow
that "all" could mean somehow
Christ's salvation is universal?

1 Corinthians 15:22

The Baptized Dead

I may not understand what Paul said,
much of it goes right over my head,
but I would like to see
when I watch my TV
a show 'bout zombies: The Baptized Dead.

1 Corinthians 15: 29

Tell Me, Death

Now when the final trumpet blasts ring
at the conclusion of everything,
tell me, Death, and quickly,
where is your victory;
where is the pain of your dreaded sting?

1 Corinthians 15: 52–55

Socialist Tendency

Though it offend Christian bourgeoisie,
it must be admitted presently
that the Apostle Paul
had the nerve and the gall

to flaunt a socialist tendency.

2 Corinthians 8: 13–15

Socialist Paul

"Give your surplus to their poverty
so that there might be equality"?!
What the hell are these marks,
the Gospel of Karl Marx?
Socialist Paul's an atrocity!

2 Corinthians 8:14

Giorgio A. Tsoukalos Explains Paul's Vision

It wasn't a bacchanalian
bout left him tatterdemalion,
but in his flesh or no
to heaven he did go.
How'd it happen? It was aliens. . .

2 Corinthians 12: 2–4

Thorn in the Flesh

Lest I should get a big head, a thorn
was given to me. I was forlorn.
Once, twice, three times I prayed.
I was, each time, dismayed
that it was still with me every morn.

2 Corinthians 12: 7–8

Galatians

Paul Emasculating his Enemies

Paul was pissed with those who were pushin'
gentile Christians to circumcision.
What he said had some sting,
"Go on! Cut the whole thing,
and not just that damned bit of foreskin!"

Galatians 5: 12

The Marks of Jesus

I've something to ask, I just gotta'
should the marks be *desiderata*?
Did Paul, on his body,
have wounds for all to see?
What exactly were these stigmata?

Galatians 6:17

Ephesians

Byzantine

Ephesians one, verse three through fourteen,
is the worst sentence I've ever seen:
pleonastic clauses
with no room for pauses. . .
Paul's writing style is byzantine.

Ephesians 1: 3–14

If it was Paul who wrote it, after all. It has been acknowledged by biblical scholars since the 1500s that the Epistle to the Ephesians has a marked difference in style from the other letters of Paul. This, combined with a borrowing of ideas and phrases, "and on occasion whole sentences" from the letter to the Colossians, leads many scholars to question whether the Apostle Paul wrote the letter to the faithful saints at Ephesus.[1]

No Coarse Joking or Foolish Talk!

Of coarse joking, Paul was a critic,
"Don't be foolish," he said. "Don't be sick."
And just what would he say
to express his dismay
at these damned biblical limericks?

Ephesians 5: 4

1. Furnish, "Ephesians, Epistle." 536.

No Pants

By breastplate and helmet we're enhanced,
a belt and shoes will improve our stance,
but what covers our legs?
Paul, answer me I begs:
the armor of God includes no pants!

Ephesians 6: 14–17

Philippians

Preaching from Partisanship

Some who preach Christ are by spite inflamed;
they suppose that by this I am maimed.
But the joke is on them,
even in their mayhem
I will rejoice that Christ is proclaimed.

Philippians 1: 15–18

Mutilation

Paul's letter is a celebration
but into this joy breaks damnation.
He raises the alarm
of those who would do harm:
Beware the Dogs of Mutilation!

Philippians 3: 2

Beware of the Dog

Finally, my brethren, I condemn
the evil workers causing mayhem,
who tear, and thrash and thresh
and mutilate the flesh,
so, my dear children, *Cave Canem!*

Philippians 3: 2

Skubalon

Paul didn't fear to let his words hit,
used words we might think too explicit,
to Philippi he wrote
a right scandalous note:
"I regard all that I've lost as shit."

Philippians 3:8

More than "rubbish," the Greek work that Paul uses means rubbish, dung, fecal matter, excrement, feces, crap.

Poor Syzygus

When Euodia and Syntyche
fought t'was best to say out of their way.
Still, Paul wanted no fuss–
sent loyal Syzygus. . .
We haven't heard from him to this day.

Philippians 4: 2–3

Colossians

Anonymous

There are scholars who would inform us
that some works in the Pauline corpus
may not be from Paul's hand;
the letter Colossians
might be the work of Anonymous.

Can I or Can't I?

Read Colossians one, and you'll conclude
that God's invisible, can't be viewed.
Other scripture verses
appear to reverse this:
you *can* see him, but then you're just screwed.

Colossians 1: 15, Exodus 33: 20

Delusions of Grandeur

I know the apostle Paul was tough,
but perhaps he's speaking off the cuff
to suggest his flesh could,
all to the church's good,
complete Christ's pains, if they weren't enough.

Colossians 1: 24

First and Second Thessalonians

Wife or Ween, Which Is It?

This next verse is something quite special:
Paul says, "Keep control of your vessel,"
but by this does he mean
rule my wife or my ween?
Figuring this out could prove stressful.

The Greek word Paul uses means "a vessel" or "an implement."
Whether Paul intended that the reader should know ow to master
his wife or his own body has been a debate among interpreters
since the early Church Fathers.[1]

1 Thessalonians 4: 4

Let the Reader Understand

Don't let yourself get down in the dump
the Last Day is still over the hump.
First the Falling Away,
then the terrible day
when the Lawless One comes with a Trump.

2 Thessalonians 2: 1–4

1. Baily, "Exegesis." 294

First and Second Timothy

Even Women Can Be Saved

Within Paul's writing there is a dearth
of good things for the women of Earth,
but continue in love
and they can be sure of
their salvation through childbirth.

1 Timothy 2: 15

Evangelic Gaudium

This command from the Apostle Paul's pen
is often ignored by wealthy men:
Don't be vain. Don't you dare,
but be willing to share;
redistribute wealth for an amen.

1 Timothy 6: 17–19

The Last Days

I wish Paul could have been more precise
about the "last days" and all their vice,
for some, to our dismay,
insist he meant today,
and no other reading will suffice.

2 Timothy 3: 1–5

God Breathed Does not Mean Inerrant

Those who claim the Bible's inerrant
say it is "God breathed" so that it can't
make a mistake or err,
but God breathed his own air
in Adam, and he weren't impeccant.

2 Timothy 3: 16, Genesis 2: 7

P.S. Can You Bring Me My Coat and Scrolls?

Do your best, and come to me quickly.
Demas, the punk, has deserted me;
Crescens and Titus too,
like witless birds they flew;
now I'm stuck with Luke to assist me.

2 Timothy 4: 9–11

Titus

Slow Bellied Gluttons

We know what is said of the Cretans,
mentally undeveloped cretins,
as their own prophet said,
they're right out of their heads,
they're liars, and slow-bellied gluttons.

Titus 1:12

Philemon

Stop Pretending

When they try to Philemon defend
some will go to great lengths to pretend
the letter does not say
that slavery's okay,
but don't they look foolish in the end?

Philemon

Hebrews

You Big Baby!

We have much that we'd like to explain
but you are stubborn and will not deign
from ignorance to turn
and you are slow to learn;
when will you begin to use your brain?

Hebrews 5: 11

Remember the Tortured

Do not forget those who have been thrust
in secret prisons, tied up and trussed.
Their pains we remember
as to our own members;
their torturers are abusing us.

Hebrews 13: 3

James

What I Really Want Is. . .

The testing of faith brings endurance.
Now, if I were asked my preference,
I would say fortitude
is a fine attitude,
but what I really want is hot-pants.

James 1:3

For Joel Watts

Go Ahead, Cut the Minimum Wage!

Listen rich people, listen and weep
for the anguish that on you now creeps;
your wealth has been foiled,
your clothes, moths have spoiled!
You won't pay fair wages. You're too cheap!

James 5: 1

First and Second Peter

I Think We Have Time

Peter said the end of all is near,
but you and I, we aren't ones to fear;
it's been quite a long spell
so I say, 'what the hell,
I think we have time to share a beer.'

1 Peter 4: 7

What Will Become of Them?

If it's hard, not just for beginners,
but for the righteous to be winners,
then we need to question
with proper discretion,
what will become of the damned sinners?

1 Peter 4: 18

Noah Was a Jerk

Peter called him a preacher righteous,
but Noah seems just a bit lifeless.
Abram, at least, argued,
would Sodom have rescued;
Noah left the world as detritus.

2 Peter 2: 5

Yeah, I Don't Understand Him, Either

Brother Paul wrote notes of instruction
that confuse as if t'were their function;
they're hard to comprehend
and some ignorant men
do distort them and cause destruction.

2 Peter 3: 15–16

First, Second and Third John

Why We Hate Them

Children, there's much we need to discuss;
this letter is not superfluous:
the Antichrist will come,
indeed there's more than one,
and we hate them 'cause they came from us.

1 John 2: 18–19

Jude

Hey Jude!

Though his sources weren't canonical
and he veers to the angelical,
your choice to avoid Jude
'cause of quotes from the psued-
epigrapha is just comical.

Jude 14

Revelation

Stop Saying Revelations!

To avoid the scholar's damnation
when making a Bible citation,
it's important to note
when copying your quote,
there is only one Revelation.

Maybe it Was Sign Language

Even on Patmos, John would rejoice;
on the Lord's Day he heard a strange noise,
like a trumpet of brass,
but a question I ask:
just how does one turn to *see* a *voice*?

Revelation 1: 12

He Wore What?!

For some it is a stubborn hurdle,
and others, it makes their blood curdle,
to imagine that our
Jesus, Lord and Savior,
would ever be dressed in a girdle.

Revelation 1: 13 (KJV)

Night and Day

Heaven's seraphim, all day and night,
sing out constantly with great might:
"Thrice holy is our king,"
though that is a strange thing
since heaven has no night, only light.

Revelation 4:8, 22:5

The Four Horsemen

The White Rider came with bow in hand.
The Red Rider took peace from the land.
The Black Rider was third,
famine was his first word;
the Green Rider is Death, ain't he grand?

Revelation 6: 1–7

Martyr Quota

Heaven won't be short one iota
so we'll have to delay the coda.
Those who were slain will wait
to receive their full fate
till the world fills its martyr quota.

Revelation 6: 9–11

Relevant, Schmelevent

If Revelation was relevant
to the people to whom it was sent,
the Mark of the Beast's not,
despite what we've been taught,

a microchip from the government.

Revelation 13: 16–18

Why I Avoid the Internet

To understand John's strange number you
treble the sixth letter in Hebrew,
then, you will see, I'll bet
why I avoid the net:
Hebrew's sixth letter is "W."

Revelation 13: 18

Hexakosioihexekontahexaphobia

Jessica has some strange nervous ticks
that her psychologist cannot fix;
she's tried medication
to cure her fixation.
She fears the number six sixty six.

Revelation 13: 17–18

Tel Megiddo

Come with me, I have something to show,
up the hill, to see Tel Megiddo,
here where cities were built,
and where much blood was spilt,
where warring, apocalyptic kings go.

Revelation 16: 16

Not So Biblical Limericks

His Wonders To Perform

Though you should read the Bible for days
you will not find that popular phrase,
and I want it noted,
the Bible's misquoted:
"The Lord works in mysterious ways. . ."

This phrase comes, not from the Bible, but from William Cowper's
hymn, "Light Shining out of Darkness"

Lilith

Before there was Eve there was Lilith,
if we believe the old Jewish myth;
when Adam approached her
to biblically know her
she fled to the desert forthwith.

Only One Syllable Difference

Of all things eschatological
the rapture is most illogical,
and we should, each one, pray
that it gets flushed away
for it's merely scatological.

We Shall Be Changed

When the rapture comes for me and you
what changes will our bodies go through?
Maybe I'm cynical;
we're told it's physical,
but what happens to our pee and poo?

Ave Maria

Hail Mary, you are so full of grace,
blessed more than other girls of our race,
blessed too is thy womb's fruit;
pray for us sinners rude,
now and as we look death in the face.

Amen

The Immaculate Conception

Was she immaculately conceived
as Catholics, of Mary, believe,
and if so, how far back
should this sinlessness track;
what womb could this perfection receive?

Inerrancy

If we're going to be coherent,
it should be readily apparent
with the contradictions,
edits, and additions,
that the Bible is not inerrant.

It's not Condemned Anywhere in the Bible

Even though most would think it taboo,
I have read the Bible through and through.
Nowhere does it condemn
my cannibalism.
I cannot kill, but I can eat you. . .

A Limerick for Emil Brunner and Karl Barth

Brunner and Barth's friendship was defunct,
all past camaraderie now junked,
and the source of their hate
was scholarly debate
pertaining to the *Anknüpfungspunkt.*

Bibliography

Baily, John, W. "1 Thessalonians: Exegesis." In *The Interpreter's Bible Volume XI*. Nashville, TN: Abingdon. 1955.

Brown, Raymond E. *The Birth of the Messiah: A Commentary on the Infancy Narratives in the Gospels of Matthew and Luke*, New York: Doubleday. 1993.

————. *The Gospel According to Johns I – XII: Introduction, Translation, and Notes*. Garden City, NY: Doubleday and Company, Inc., 1966.

Crenshaw, James L. "Proverbs, Book of." In *The Anchor Bible Dictionary Volume V*, edited by David Noel Freedman et al., New York: Doubleday. 1992.

Di Lella, Alexander A. "Wisdom of Ben-Sira." In *The Anchor Bible Dictionary Volume VI*, edited by David Noel Freedman et al., New York: Doubleday. 1992.

Furnish, Victor Paul. "Ephesians, Epistle to the" In *The Anchor Bible Dictionary Volume II*, edited by David Noel Freedman et al., New York: Doubleday. 1992.

Gilad, Elon. "How Isaiah Gave Hebrew Its Word for Vagina." *Haaretz* September 1, 2015. http://www.haaretz.com/jewish-world/jewish-world-features/.premium-1.673930

Grant, Frederick C., "The Gospel According to Mark: Exegesis" In *The Interpreter's Bible Volume VII*, edited by George Arthur Buttrick et al., Nashville, TN: Abingdon. 1951.

González, Justo L. *The Story of Christianity: The Early Church to the Present Day*. Peabody: MA, 1984.

Hooker, Morna D. *Beginnings: Keys that Open the Gospels*. Harrisburg, PA: Trinity Press International. 1997.

Katzenstein, H. J. "Tyre." In *The Anchor Bible Dictionary Volume VI*, edited by David Noel Freedman et al., New York: Doubleday. 1992.

Lampe, Peter. "Junias." In *The Anchor Bible Dictionary Volume III*, edited by David Noel Freedman et al., New York: Doubleday. 1992.

Mann, C. S. *Mark: A New Translation with Introduction and Commentary*, Garden City, NY: Doubleday and Company, Inc., 1984.

Myers, Jacob M. *I Chronicles: Introduction, Translation, and Notes*, Garden City, NY: Doubleday. 1974.

Neev, David, and K. O. Emery. *The Destruction of Sodom, Gomorrah, and Jericho: Geological, Climatological, and Archaeological Background*, New York: Oxford University Press, 1995.

Pope, Marvin H. "Euphemism and Dysphemism in the Bible." In *The Anchor Bible Dictionary Volume I*, edited by David Noel Freedman et al., New York: Doubleday. 1992.

Robertson, A. T. *Word Pictures in the New Testament Volume I*, Nashville, TN: Broadman. 1930.

Simundson, Daniel J. "Micah." In *The New Interpreter's Bible Volume VII*, edited by Leander E Keck et al., Nashville, TN: Abingdon 1996.

Thayer, Joseph Henry, *Thayer's Greek-English Lexicon of the New Testament*. Grand Rapids, MI: Associated Publishers and Authors Inc., 1889

Thiselton, Anthony C. "Can Hermeneutics Ease the Deadlock? Some Biblical Exegesis and Hermeneutical Models," In *The Way Forward? Christian Voices on Homosexuality and the Church*. Edited by Timothy Bradshaw. Grand Rapids, MI: William B. Eerdmans. 2003.

Weems, Renita J. *Battered Love: Marriage, Sex, and Violence in the Hebrew Prophets*, Minneapolis, MN: Ausburg Fortress. 1995.

CPSIA information can be obtained
at www.ICGtesting.com
Printed in the USA
BVOW08*1944260318
511391BV00011B/11/P